The World in a Nutshell

Pakistan
in a nutshell

*

SCHAUMBURG TOWNSHIP DISTRICT LIBRARY
130 SOUTH ROSELLE ROAD
SCHAUMBURG, ILLINOIS 60193

Enisen Publishing

954.91
RORABACK,

3 1257 01571 1335

*FLAG: Pakistan's flag has a green background with a white band on the hoist side. The green color represents Pakistan's Islamic majority while the vertical white band symbolizes the country's non-Muslim minority population. A large white crescent and star centered in the green field are traditional symbols of Islam (as is the color green). They also represent progress and knowledge respectively.

Pakistan in a Nutshell
First edition – April 2002
First published – April 2002
Second edition – September 2004

Enisen Publishing
2118 Wilshire Boulevard #351
Santa Monica, CA 90403-5784
www.enisen.com
publishing@enisen.com

Text   Amanda Roraback
Maps   Katie Gerber
Editor   Paul Bernhard
Editor-in-Chief   Dorothy A. Roraback

Copyright © 2002, 2004 by Enisen Publishing and Nutshell Notes, LLC

All rights reserved. No part of this book may be reproduced in any form or by any means without written permission from Enisen Publishing.

Nutshell Notes and the Nutshell Notes logo are trademarks of Enisen Publishing and Nutshell Notes, LLC.

Library of Congress Control Number: 2004111753

ISBN: 0-9702908-9-6

Printed in the United States of America

TABLE OF CONTENTS

PAKISTAN AT A GLANCE

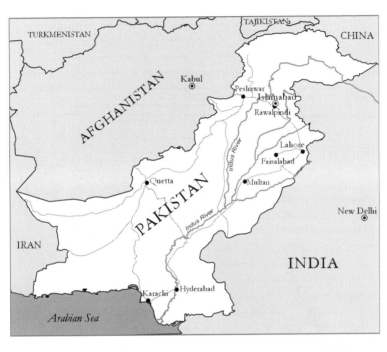

250 Kilometers

250 Miles

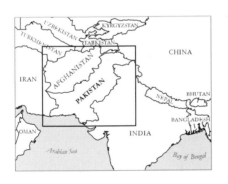

⊙	Capital City
●	Other Cities
∽	River
∽	Major Road

FACTS and FIGURES

Name: Islamic Republic of Pakistan

Capital City: Islamabad (Karachi was Pakistan's capital until 1961 when the capital was moved to the new city of Islamabad [meaning "abode of Islam"] because it was situated safely in the middle of the country next to the military town of Rawalpindi.)

Head of State: President Pervez Musharraf (next election to be held in 2007)

Population: 159,196,336 (July 2004 est.)*
Ethnic Groups: Punjabi, Sindhi, Pathan (Pashtun) Baloch and Mohajir (imigrants from India and their descendents)

Religion: Muslim 97% (composed of Sunni 77%, Shi'a 20%), Christian, Hindu, Zoroastrian and other 3%* (95% Muslim, 5% others)

Languages: National language: Urdu
Languages spoken: Punjabi 48%, Sindhi 12%, Siraiki (a Punjabi variant) 10%, Pashtu 8%, Urdu 8%, Baloch 3%, Hindko 2%, Brahui 1%, Burushaski, others, 8%*

English is the official language in most government ministries and the *lingua franca* of the Pakistani elite.
Most Pakistanis are bilingual, speaking Urdu and their regional dialect with equal fluency.

Literacy: Male: 59.8%, Female 30.6% (2003 est.*)

Currency: 1 Pakistani rupee = 100 paisa

Per Capita income $460

Foreign Debt: $36 billion (The government spends nearly 40% of its budget making payments on the national debt.)

Exports: 85% Exports – textiles (clothes, cotton cloth, yarn) also, rice, leather items, carpets, sports goods, handicrafts, chemicals.

Military: **Pakistan** Standing Army: 550,000, Defense Spending: $3.3 billion (4.2% of GDP) Principal Arms Supplier: China
India – Standing army: 1,100,000, Defense Spending: $13.94 billion (2.5% of GDP), Principal Arms Supplier: Russia
Source: Asia Time

Mountain Ranges: Pakistan is home to three of the world's great mountain ranges, Hindukush, the Himalayas and Karkorams, as well as some of the highest peaks in the world, including K-2 (28,250 feet, second only to Mt. Everest).

Sports: Hockey is the national game of Pakistan

* Figures taken from the CIA Factbook

PEOPLE AND POLICIES

GENERAL PERVEZ MUSHARRAF

Musharraf, Pakistan's Chief of Army Staff (COAS) became the country's Chief Executive following a military takeover on Oct. 12, 1999. In June he appointed himself president. His rule was legitimized in a referendum held April 30, 2002.

ISI (Inter-Services Intelligence)

Pakistan's military intelligence agency. The ISI is part of the Ministry of Defense and is headed by a Director General (always an army officer of the rank of Lieutenant General). The agency is answerable to the Prime Minister (chief executive). Military Intelligence is under the Chief of Army Staff (COAS).

LAHORE RESOLUTION (or Pakistan Resolution)

Submitted to the All-India Muslim League by Mohammed Ali Jinnah (the founder of Pakistan) in March 1940, the Lahore Resolution proposed that the areas of India in which Muslims are numerically in a majority "should be grouped to constitute Independent States."

DELHI CONVENTION RESOLUTION

Adopted by the Muslim League in April 1946, the Delhi Resolution went a step further than the **Lahore Resolution** by specifically identifying the provinces to be included in the new independent state of "Pakistan."

OBJECTIVES RESOLUTION

Passed by the Constituent Assembly of Pakistan in March 1949, the Objectives Resolution outlined Pakistan's dedication to the principles of "democracy, freedom, equality, tolerance and social justice as enunciated by Islam." The Resolution also stipulated that adequate provisions would be made for minorities to protect their right to profess and practice their religions and develop their cultures.

LINE OF CONTROL

The Line of Control divides Kashmir into Pakistani and Indian spheres of influence. The present demarcation line was drawn in 1972 as part of a cease-fire agreement between Pakistan and India.

SIMLA AGREEMENT

Signed by both India and Pakistan in 1972, the Simla Agreement committed both nations to reaching a "final settlement" on the Kashmir issue and cultivating "friendly and harmonious relations."

DURAND LINE

Designated by the British in 1863, the Durand Line marks the current border between Afghanistan and Pakistan. The boundary has been contested by Pathan tribesmen living on both sides of the line who felt that Pathans should join to form their own nation of "Pashtunistan," independent of Pakistan and Afghanistan.

MOHAJIRS
At the time of partition a number of Muslims left their homes in India to live in the Islamic homeland of Pakistan. Most of the Urdu-speaking immigrants (*Mohajirs*) had come from urban backgrounds and settled in Karachi and Hyderabad where they appropriated businesses previously managed by Hindus who had fled to India. Their domination in commercial and political affairs caused resentment among the local Sindhis. (The word "Mohajir" comes from the Islamic term *Hijr*, the flight of the prophet Mohammed from Mecca to Medina to escape to escape religious persecution).

KALASHNIKOV CULTURE
Named after the Russian assault rifle, the AK-47 or Kalashnikov, the "Kalashnikov Culture" came about as a result of the Soviet-Afghan war in the 1980s. During the war, the United States supplied resistance groups in Afghanistan (the *mujahideen* or "holy warriors") with weapons stockpiled and shipped through Peshawar in Pakistan. After the war, Peshawar was left with a mountain of surplus weapons that continued to grow as manufacturers added their own locally produced Kalashnikov replicas. Attempts to de-weaponize the area have been frustrated by the influx of Afghan warlords escaping persecution in their home country.

STRATEGIC DEPTH
A secure Afghan frontier provided Pakistan with "strategic depth" by permitting Pakistani forces to be stationed on India's border without fear of a two-front war. Safe passage through Afghanistan would also allow Pakistan to cultivate stronger political and economic ties with the Muslim Central Asian countries.

SHARIAH
"The Path." The term for Islamic law.

ABDUL QADEER KHAN
Considered the "Father of the Pakistan Bomb," Abdul Qadeer Khan headed the nation's nuclear program from the eponymous Khan Research Laboratories. In 2004, Khan admitted to having passed nuclear technology from Pakistan to other countries including North Korea, Libya and Iran.

LEGAL FRAMEWORK ORDER (LFO)
On Aug. 24, 2002, President Musharraf issued the LFO 2002 announcing "if any necessity arises for any further amendment of the Consitution... the Chief Executive will have the discretionary power to make provisions and pass orders for amending the Constitution or for removing any difficulty." Opponents claim the Order gives the President too much power in allowing him to sack a prime minister and dissolve parliament. Although amendments don't specifically give the President these powers, the controversial clause (Article 58-[2] [B]) has been misused by three Presidents in the past to remove prime ministers for purely political reasons.

BACKGROUND

ANCIENT HISTORY

Although the Islamic Republic of Pakistan has only existed half a century, the history of its people goes back to prehistoric days. One of the earliest villages in the world was uncovered in **Mehrgarh** (in Balochistan) whose inhabitants were believed to have begun using metal as early as 7000 B.C. Excavations at **Harappa** (in South Punjab) and **Moenjodaro** (in Sindh) also suggest that a highly developed civilization living in the Indus Valley region in the third millennium B.C. constructed elaborate cities with stone drainage systems, furnaces and brick houses aligned in a grid-like city layout.

In 1700 B.C. **Aryans** arrived in Pakistan from Persia introducing their Vedic religious texts, which later inspired the teachings of Hinduism and Buddhism, their caste system (a social structure in which classes are determined by heredity), and the Sanskrit language to the subcontinent.

The Aryans had invaded Balochistan, Sindh and Punjab by the time the Persian **Achaemenids** under **Cyrus the Great** (580-529 B.C.), the most powerful empire in Asia and the Middle East, had begun to extend their influence into modern-day Pakistan. The principality of **Gandhara** (which included the cities of Kabul, Peshawar and parts of the Swat valleys) became the Empire's 20th *satrapy* (province).

In 330 B.C., the Achaemenid/Persian Empire fell to the Macedonian king, **Alexander the Great,** who marched his soldiers south from Afghanistan into Punjab and down the Indus River to the Arabian Sea, establishing a number of cities along the way.

After Alexander's death in 321 B.C., one of his generals, **Seleucus**, became ruler of the eastern provinces (Bactria [Afghanistan], Iran, Iraq, Syria, Lebanon, Armenia, parts of Turkey, Uzbekistan, Turkmenistan and Tajikistan). In 304 B.C. Seleucus relinquished control of the Indus Valley (Gandhara) to an Indian ruler from the Ganges Basin, **Chandragupta Maurya** (reigned from 321 –297 B.C.), in exchange for 500 elephants—thus establishing the **Mauryan dynasty**.

By 290 BC **Chandragupta's** son **Bindusara** had expanded the Mauryan Empire to include almost all of India.

Under **Chandragupta's** grandson, **Ashoka** (or Asoka), who ascended the Mauryan throne in 260 B.C. and converted to Buddhism, Gandhara became the scene of intense Buddhist missionary activity. From Gandhara, Buddhist teachers spread the faith to Peshawar, Kabul, Kashmir and eventually to China and other cities around the world. With the death of Ashoka in 232 B.C., the Mauryan Empire broke into smaller kingdoms and eventually fell to the **Kushans** from Central Asia.

Kanishka, one of the rulers of the **Kushan Empire** that dominated parts of Turkistan, Afghanistan, Pakistan and the northern section of India in the 1st century A.D., also actively espoused the cause of Buddhism, hoping to play the part of a "second Ashoka." The Kushans, who controlled the prosperous Silk Road trade route from Rome to Xi'an, China, ruled from their winter capital in Peshawar and summer capital in Kabul until the middle of the third century A.D.

By the fourth century A.D., the Kushan Empire had disintegrated into a number of independent states fighting among themselves. For nearly a hundred years, the area languished in a state of military and political turmoil until a devout Hindu called **Chandra Gupta** consolidated the tribes and initiated the **Gupta Dynasty** in A.D. 328. By intermarriage and conquest, the Guptas expanded their power over northern India, ushering in India's golden age of religious tolerance, cultural advancement and prosperity.

Three hundred years later, the Gupta Dynasty fell prey to an invasion by the barbaric **White Huns (Hephthalites)**. The Huns, who eventually assimilated into the indigenous population and converted to Hinduism, put an end to Buddhist activity. Buddhism only emerged again in China.

ARRIVAL OF ISLAM

Islam was introduced into South Asia in the early 8th century when **Mohammed Bin Qasim** arrived from the Damascus-based **Umayyad** (Omayyid) Empire. He was the son-in-law of the Governor of Iraq who had sent him to Sindh to avenge the seizure by Sindhi pirates of an Arab ship carrying costly gifts from the King of Ceylon. From the captured seaport of Daibul, (now Banbhore), where he erected Pakistan's first mosque, Bin Qasim conquered the lower Indus Valley area (Sindh) and extended his rule north to Multan.

While the Sindhis were not coerced to convert to Islam by the Arabic invaders (proselytizing is discouraged in Islam), some lower-caste Hindus saw conversion as a means to elevate their social status and get better jobs. Mass conversions to Islam came later when the Turks based in Ghazni (in modern day Afghanistan) extended their empire through Pakistan to the borders of India in the 10th century and made Islam the state religion.

By the time the Turkish Sultan **Mahmud of Ghazni** concluded his incursion into the area, the **Ghaznavid Empire** had incorporated the states of Gandhara, Punjab, Sindh and Balochistan and established the city of Lahore as an Islamic cultural center.

At the end of the 12th century, the Muslims conquered the rest of India under the Turkish **Sultan Mohammed of Ghor** (or Ghaur) who had overthrown the Ghaznavid Empire from his base at Ghor in Afghanistan. In 1192, the Sultan captured Delhi and by 1202 he had conquered the most powerful

Hindu kingdoms along the Ganges River, launching the 300-year **Sultanate Period** in India-Pakistan history.

As the Muslim sultans conquered the areas of Pakistan and northern India and converted the population by the sword, **Sufi** Muslim mystics were spreading the religion peacefully through the sub-continent. The tolerant, spiritual Sufi presentation of Islam helped to overcome differences between Islam and Hinduism and even fired the imagination of Hindu reformers who envisioned a synthesis of both religions.

Because of the Sufi influence, Islam remained the religion of the majority only on the western and eastern peripheries of India where the mystics were most active—the areas that would eventually become West and East Pakistan.

THE MOGHUL EMPIRE

Early in the 16th century, **Zahir-ud-Din Babur**, a descendant of both **Tamerlane** (Timur) and **Genghiz Khan,** established himself in Afghanistan where he began to lay the foundations for a line of Muslim emperors known as the **Moghuls.** From Afghanistan, Babur raided Punjab and two years later in 1526 defeated the Delhi Sultans. By the end of the 16th century, the empire extended from the Arabian Sea to Bengal (present-day Bangladesh) and from Kashmir to the Deccan Plateau in India.

Moghul rule was further consolidated by **Akbar,** the greatest Moghul emperor, who enhanced relations between Hindus and Muslims by ending the supremacy of Islam as the state religion, abolishing the *jizya*, a special tax levied on Hindus, and marrying many Hindu wives.

Akbar's great grandson, **Aurangzeb** (1658-1707) wasn't nearly as tolerant. The deeply pious Moghul ruler banned music and the use of alcohol and opium at court, re-imposed heavy taxes on non-Muslims and returned the state to strict orthodox Islamic rule. The Sikhs, who had prospered under Akbar, began to organize themselves as a warrior tribe in retaliation.

SIKHS

Sikhism, a synthesis of Sufism and Hinduism based on the teaching of **Baba Guru Nanak,** was established in Punjab in the late 15th century. The Sikhs contributed to the downfall of the Moghul Empire after the death of Aurangzeb by staging uprisings against a government that was already crippled by chaos and foreign invasion.

At the end of the 18th century, the most powerful of the Sikh leaders, **Maharaja Ranjit Singh** (1799-1839), united Punjab under his rule, declared Lahore the capital and created one of the mightiest armies in the subcontinent. By the time of his death in 1839, his army had pushed back the Afghans (who had been making inroads into Pakistan under **Ahmed Shah Durrani,** the founder of Afghanistan) and incorporated Kashmir, Ladakh, Baltistan, Gilgit, Hazara and the Peshawar Valley into the Sikh Empire.

THE BRITISH

The British began arriving in the subcontinent of India at the beginning of the 17th century as merchants working with the **British East India Company.** As the power of the **Moghuls** declined, foreign influence increased until the East India Company, eventually run by the British government, was calling the shots. The British then began to annex Indian territories one by one by offering local Indian rulers protection and subsidies for their loyalty. In 1857, an uprising (called the **Sepoy Mutiny** by the West and the **1st War of Independence** by Pakistan) compelled the British to disband the Company and take full control over India. Two hundred years after they arrived on the continent, the colonists controlled most of India and began setting their sights on the northwestern territories that now make up Pakistan.

BRITISH IN PUNJAB AND KASHMIR

As long as **Ranjit Singh** reigned in Punjab, the British honored an agreement they had made with the Sikh leader at the beginning of the 19th century to leave his empire alone. Less than a decade after his 1839 death, however, the British became engaged in two brief but bloody wars with the Sikhs and won control over Punjab and the northwest.

To reward one of Ranjit Singh's commanders, **Gulab Singh**—a Hindu—for helping the British defeat his former allies, they granted him the areas of Kashmir, Ladakh, Baltistan and Gilgit (which they renamed the State of **Jammu and Kashmir**). Under the **Treaty of Amritsar**, the Maharajah (Prince **Gulab Singh**) and his descendents were given control over Jammu and Kashmir under British sovereignty for a yearly payment of one shawl and 100 goats.

BRITISH IN SINDH

Seeing commercial and strategic value in the Indus River area, the British persuaded the rulers of Sindh, the **Mirs of Talpur,** into opening up the river for international passage with the provision that no armed vessels would be permitted to use the waterway. In 1839, the British violated their own proviso and ushered troops along the Indus to fight a war in Afghanistan. The Sindhis fought the British imperialists but couldn't prevent Britain from annexing the territory in 1846.

BRITISH IN NORTHWEST FRONTIER PROVINCE

The Russian encroachment into central Asia after the **Crimean War** in 1853 threatened Britain's northwest frontier. In 1879, the British attempted to foil Russia's advances by installing one of their own favorites on the

Afghanistan throne. When that plan failed, they instead negotiated with the Afghan ruler to draw a common border between the two countries. The so-called 1893 **Durand Line** between British India and Afghanistan was drawn right through **Pathan** (Pashtun) territory, igniting Pathan revolts. Seeing the impracticality of ruling the area as part of Punjab, Viceroy to India **Lord Curzon** created the "North West Frontier Province (NWFP)" and granted the fierce Pathan tribes almost complete autonomy in the Tribal Areas, a system that was also followed by the current Pakistan government.

BRITISH IN BALOCHISTAN

To the west, Balochistan, with its border alongside Persia and Afghanistan, was also of vital importance to the British who wanted to create a cushion of friendly buffer states between their Indian empire and Russia. In 1866, the colonists appointed **Robert Sandeman** to pacify the fiercely independent tribal leaders, the *sardars*. He promised them British support while recruiting small forces of tribal horsemen for local policing. Through diplomatic and manipulative methods, Balochistan formally became a British territory in 1887.

SEEDS OF PARTITION

By the end of the 19th century, Britain's Asian empire extended from the edge of Afghanistan to the border of China, and the local power had shifted away from the Muslims—who had ruled the subcontinent for the past seven centuries—to the Hindus. In 1885, the local population was permitted by the British to form an indigenous **Indian National Congress,** ostensibly to provide representation for all Indians. In truth, the organization carried a strong anti-Islamic bias, prompting Muslims to form their own party, the **All-Indian Muslim League**, in 1906.

Far from being antagonistic, however, members of the Muslim League often were also affiliated with the **Indian National Congress** and were welcomed by Hindu Congress members. This fluidity made it easy for the parties to come together a decade later (1916) to sign the **Lucknow Pact** in order to more effectively fight for their common goal of independence from British colonists.

For the next decade the cause of liberation was propelled by an alliance of three remarkable men: **Mohandas Gandhi**, as ascetic Hindu lawyer who was determined to lead India to independence through non-violent passive resistance, **Jawaharlal Nehru**, the head of the Congress Party, and **Mohammad Ali Jinnah**, who led the Muslim League.

However, by the time India's independence looked inevitable, the Hindu-Muslim alliance had fallen apart. Congress leaders had ignored Muslim demands, Muslim League members objected to perceived Hindu arrogance, and Jinnah, who had become discouraged by Gandhi's extralegal tactics, had left the country.

While living in self-imposed exile in England, the future father of Pakistan (Quaid-i-Azam), Jinnah, had become inspired by poet **Allama Mohammed Iqbal** who had drawn up a proposal for a separate Muslim homeland in northwest India, and adopted the acronym "P.A.K.I.S.T.A.N." coined by a group of Muslim exiles at Cambridge University as the country's new name. (see introduction)

When he returned to India in 1935, Jinnah reinvigorated the Muslim League with a new and more impassioned mission. Claiming that "Islam was in danger," Jinnah convinced the Muslim League to pass the **Lahore** (or **Pakistan**) **Resolution** in 1940 demanding a separate Muslim state.

In an atmosphere of violence as Muslims and Hindus turned on each other, the new British viceroy, **Lord Louis Mountbatten** recognized that the only way to prevent anarchy was to give in to Jinnah's demands. Mountbatten announced that Pakistan would receive independence by August 14, 1947.

PARTITION: CHOOSING SIDES

Indians were given a choice —join either the new Muslim state of Pakistan (divided into West Pakistan and East Pakistan which would include Bengal), or predominantly Hindu India. Balochistan, the North West Frontier Province and Sindh voted to join Pakistan without much incident. Indians from Punjab and Bengal, however, faced greater difficulties since those areas were home to a mixed population of Hindus, Muslims and Sikhs. Lines determined by **Sir Cyril Radcliffe** were drawn arbitrarily dividing the provinces in half, resulting in the greatest migration in human history. Sikhs and Hindus emigrated from the Pakistan portion of Punjab and Bengal into India as Muslims moved in the other direction. Hundreds of thousands of people were killed in the fighting that occurred along the way.

The seeds of the ongoing **Kashmir** crisis were also sown during this period of independence and partition (see chapter on Kashmir).

On August 14, 1947, the flag of Pakistan was flown for the first time in the country's new capital of Karachi and Mohammed Ali Jinnah headed the nation as Governor General.

ANCIENT HISTORY TIMELINE

3000 - 1500 BC	Indus Valley Civilization	Moenjodaro, Harappa, Kot Diji, Mehrgarh
1700 BC	Aryans	Vedic religion and Sanskrit introduced
550-330 BC	Achaemenids	Gandhara is 20th satrapy
327 BC	Alexander the Great (d.323)	
304-185 BC	Mauryan Rule	
260-232 BC	Ashoka	Gandhara becomes center of Buddhism
50 - 250 AD	Kushan Dynasty	Rulers of Kushan Empire maintain contacts with Rome
318 - 550 AD	Gupta Dynasty in India	Golden Age of Indian Culture
455 AD	White Huns (Hepthalites)	White Huns convert to Hinduism, destroyed Buddhist monasteries
711-712	Mohammed bin Qasim	Islam first introduced to Pakistan
1021-1186	Ghaznavids	Son of Turkish slave king from Afghanistan (Sultan Mahood of Ghazni)
1186-1192	Ghauris (or Ghoris)	Turkish Sultan Mohammed of Ghaur
1192-1524	Sultans	Delhi replaces Lahore as seat of Muslim administration
1524-1764	Moghul Dynasty	Zahir-ud Din Babur
1556-1605	Akbar	Enhanced relations between Hindus and Muslims
1658 - 1707	Aurangzeb	Return to strict Muslim Orthodox rule
1747	Ahmed Shah Durrani	Founded kingdom of Afghanistan
1799 - 1839	Ranjit Sikh	1819 Siege of Multan
1845-1846	1st British-Sikh War	British annex Sindh
1848-1849	2nd British-Sikh War	British take Punjab
1857-1858	Sepoy Mutiny (War of Independence)	
1893	Durand Line drawn	
1885	National Congress founded	
1887	Balochistan becomes British territory	
1906	All-India Muslim League founded	North West Frontier Province created
1916	Lucknow Pact	
1930-1935	Jinnah in Britain	1933 "Now or Never" (Rehmat Ali)
1940	Lahore Resolution	
1946	Delhi Resolution	
1947	Independence and Partition	

MODERN HISTORY TIMELINE

Year	Gov. Gen/Other	President	Prime Minister	Internal Affairs	Foreign Affairs
1947	Jinnah		Liaquat Ali Khan		1st war with India over Kashmir
1948	Nazimuddin				Ghandi assassinated
1949				Objectives Resolution	UN cease-fire over Kashmir
1951	Ghulam Mohammed		Nazimuddin		
1952				Demonstrations in Bangladesh over language	
1953			Mohammad Ali Bogra		
1955	Mirza		Chauhdry Mohammad Ali		
1956		Mirza	Suhrawardy	Pakistan declared Islamic republic	
1958		Ayub Khan		Martial Law	
1965					Nehru dies; 2nd war with India
1969		Yahya Khan		Martial Law	
1970				1st general election, Awami League wins	
1971		Z.A. Bhutto		Civil War with Bangladesh	3rd war with India over Bangladesh
1972					Simla Agreement with India
1973		F.E. Chaudhry	Z.A. Bhutto	Insurgence in Balochisatan	Sardar Daud in power in Afghanistan
1974				Anti-Ahmadi bill	India's first nuclear tests
1977	Zia ul-Haq (Martial Law Administrator)			Introduction of Federal Shariat Court	
1978		Zia ul-Haq		Martial Law	
1979				Islamic Penal Code	Soviets invade Afghanistan
1983				Sindhis rise up	
1984		Ghulam Ishaq Khan	('85) M.K. Junejo		Siachen Glacier skirmish in Kashmir
1988			Benazir Bhutto		
1990			Nawaz Sharif		
1993		Farooq Leghari	Benazir Bhutto		
1997		Wasim Sajjad	Nawaz Sharif		
1998		Rafiq Tarar		Pakistan tests Ghauri Missile	International sanctions imposed
1999	P. Musharraf				Kargil skirmish in Kashmir
2001		P. Musharraf			Terrorist attacks in NYC, Afghanistan war
2002			Mir Zafarullah Khan Jamali		
2004			Chaudhry Shujaat Hussain /Shaukat Aziz		('03) US/Br. War in Iraq

P.A.K.I.S.T.A.N

While the first documented proposal for an independent Muslim federation was made in 1930 by poet-philosopher Dr. Allama Mohammed Iqbal, it was the work of **Chadhri (or Chowdhry) Rehmat Ali** and a group of Muslim exiles at Cambridge University in England who gave the country its acronymic name.

The Muslim federation, as described by Rehmat Ali in his 1933 book Now or Never; Are We to Live or Perish Forever?, would include the five northern units of India including Punjab, Afghania Province (North West Frontier Province), Kashmir, Sindh and Balochistan. Ali coined the name "PAKSTAN," or "land of the pure" in Urdu, by joining initials from each territory and adding Balochistan's suffix- stan which means "place where one stays": from the Iranian root "st " (as in Afghanistan, Turkmenistan, Kurdistan etc.)

Ali's original acronym was later expanded to "P.A.K.I.S.T.A.N" to include neighboring territories with high concentrations of Muslims that he considered part of the original Fatherland. The letters came to represent the following regions:

Punjab   (Including the portion that now lies within India's borders)
Afghania   (The original name for the North West Frontier Province)
Kashmir   (All of Kashmir)
Iran
Sindh   (including Kahch and Kathiawar)
Tukharistan   (The area of Turkmenistan and Central Asian states)
Afghanistan   UPA-GANA-STAN-(Sanskrit: place inhabited by allied tribes)
BalochistaN

The name was adopted and used in the 1930s and 40s by members of the Muslim League when they discussed plans for the future of the subcontinent. The name's creator, however, received little recognition. **Rehmat Ali** returned to Pakistan after its formation as a country in 1947 but was exiled back to England a few months later where he died in poverty.

POLITICAL BIOGRAPHIES

MOHAMMED ALI JINNAH—Governor-General (1947-1948)
Jinnah, Pakistan's "Quaid-i-Azam" or "Father of the Nation," helped orchestrate Pakistan's liberation from India in 1947 as president of the Muslim League.

Considered the "best ambassador of Hindu-Muslim unity," he initially bridged relations between India's Hindu-prominent Congress Party and the All-India Muslim League in the early 1920s, but broke with Congress a few years later, deeming their approach toward independence unconstitutional and essentially Hindu in nature. After a 5-year self-imposed exile in England, where he became inspired by poet **Mohammed Iqbal's** proposal of a separate Muslim homeland, he returned to India and reinvigorated the **Muslim League** – this time with the mission of creating a separate Muslim state called "Pakistan."

In recognition of Jinnah's 1940 **Lahore Resolution**, which stated that Muslims should be a separate nation, Britain, under the administration of **British Viceroy Lord Mountbatten**, announced that Pakistan would receive its independence in August 1947. Fourteen months later, Mohammed Ali Jinnah, Pakistan's first Governor General, died of tuberculosis and was succeeded by **Khwaja Nazimuddin**, with **Liaquat Ali Khan** continuing as Prime Minister.

LIAQUAT ALI KHAN —Prime Minister (1947-1951)
Like Jinnah, Liaquat Ali Khan was also a moderate who believed that Pakistan should be run as a democratic, secular state. In March 1949, he helped pass Pakistan's **Objectives Resolution**, which defined Pakistan as a Muslim state dedicated to the principles of democracy, freedom, equality, tolerance and social justice as outlined in the Quran.

When **Khan** was assassinated in 1951, **Khwaja Nazimuddin** stepped down as Governor General to serve as Pakistan's second prime minister. **Ghulam Mohammed** became Governor General.

KHWAJA NAZIMUDDIN —Governor General (1948-1951), Prime Minister (1951-1953)
Nazimuddin served as the Chief Minister of East Bengal from the creation of Pakistan until **Jinnah's** death in September, 1948, at which point he became the Governor General. After **Liaquat Ali Khan** was assassinated on October 16, 1951, Nazimuddin became the Prime Minister. A year later, he publicly declared that Urdu alone would be the state language, angering the citizens of East Bengal (whose first language was Bangla) and setting off the Bengalese drive for independence from the rest of Pakistan.

Nazimuddin was removed from office in 1953 by Governor General **Ghulam Mohammed.**

GHULAM MOHAMMED —Governor General (1951-1955)
Seven years after Pakistan's creation, the government still had not produced a constitution nor outlined plans to deal with the country's regional and sectarian differences. The impasse prompted Ghulam Mohammed to dismiss the **Constituent Assembly** (Pakistan's legislature) in 1954. A year later he resigned because of poor health and was replaced by **Iskander Mirza**.

ISKANDER MIRZA —Governor General (1955-56), President (1956-58)
Under Iskander Mirza the new Constituent Assembly promulgated Pakistan's first constitution, making Pakistan officially an "Islamic Republic" and replacing the office of Governor General with a presidency. Adhering to the new terms, Mirza became president in 1956. But soon after, he abrogated the constitution, disbanded the Legislative Assembly and declared martial law to curb the rampant ethnic, religious and political instability that plagued the country.

In 1958, **Mirza** was toppled in a coup d'etat staged by Pakistan's first Commander-in-Chief, General **Mohammed Ayub Khan**.

GENERAL AYUB KHAN (1958-1969)
Soon after authoritarian Ayub Khan assumed the presidency, he purged the government of civilian politicians, replacing them with army officers. He also initiated a plan for "**Basic Democracies**," a multi-tiered pyramidal hierarchy that distributed power from the local level to the top political echelons.

The "Basic Democrats," (80,000 Pakistanis elected from local villagers), were asked to endorse Ayub Khan's presidency and approve his new constitution, which called for a weakened legislature and strong presidency.

By the end of the 1960s, Ayub Khan had lost most of his support and handed over power to the Commander-in-Chief, General **Agha Muhammad Yahya Khan**. The constitution that Ayub Khan had implemented in 1962 was annulled soon after.

GENERAL YAHYA KHAN (1969-1971)
When Yahya Khan came to power he established a semi-military state and restructured representation in the government's legislative assembly according to population size, giving East Pakistan—which was more ethnically homogeneous and politically unified— a huge advantage. When East Pakistan's **Awami League** won 167 of 300 seats in the elections of 1970, West Pakistani politicians rose up in fury and refused to be a part of Bengali-dominated assembly. Although Yahya Khan desperately tried to hold the country together, the ensuing strikes and revolts in the east forced him to declare the elections void. He handed over authority to **Zulfikar Ali Bhutto**, who's **Pakistan People's Party** (PPP) had won the majority of seats in West Pakistan.

ZULFIKAR ALI BHUTTO—President (1971-1973), Prime Minister (1973-1977)

The independence of **Bangladesh** (see "Bangladesh" section) and ensuing regional instability upon Bhutto's accession to the presidency shaped much of the country's future political activity. Bhutto tried to bridge the gap that had grown between the center (a federal government perceived to be dominated by wealthy Punjabis) and the peripheries by giving more legislative representation and power to local politicians. At the same time, he wielded a heavy hand against provincial opposition and resistance to his programs, especially in Balochistan. He also reduced the power of the landlords (*zamindars*) and the country's corporate, financial and bureaucratic elite by introducing a series of socialist reforms.

Under the terms of his new constitution of 1973, Islam was declared the state religion and power was shifted from the president to the prime minister, the office Bhutto assumed the same year.

When Z.A. Bhutto's Pakistan People's Party won an overwhelming victory in the 1977 elections, his opposition—which had been deprived of power under Bhutto's legislation— charged him with rigging the elections and launched mass disturbances that required the army to quell. To restore law and order, the military deposed Bhutto, installed **Zia ul-Haq** and imposed martial law. Bhutto was hanged two years later for allegedly ordering the murder of a political opponent.

MAJOR GENERAL MOHAMAD ZIA UL-HAQ—Martial Law Administrator (1977),President (1978-1988)

Chief of Army Staff Zia ul-Haq, who was installed as Martial Law administrator after the coup of 1977, spent most of his administration trying to demonstrate his legitimacy as Pakistan's head of state.

Immediately after taking control, the new government declared martial law, arrested thousands of PPP supporters, and suspended the constitution, ostensibly to create a stable environment in which fair elections could be held. The promised elections, however, didn't take place for another eight years.

Zia declared, furthermore, that Pakistan's survival and progress depended on the realization of its purpose as a Muslim state. Through his ardent "Islamization" program, the President implemented a number of policies to bring the political structure, economic system, law and society into conformity with Islamic principles. His reputation as a defender of Islam was cemented with Pakistan's involvement in the war against the Soviets in Afghanistan in the 1980s. Moreover, with the influx of foreign aid from the US to help in the war effort, Pakistan's economy grew steadily.

While Zia tried to redirect attention from his questionable ascendancy with visions of Islamic purity, he also tried to silence opposition within the government. In Zia's revised **Constitution of 1981,** the legislature was reduced to an advisory body and the president alone determined the extent of his powers. It was the president, not Parliament, who would be responsible for choosing a prime minister (Zia selected **Mohammed Khan Junejo).** And by invoking the **8th amendment,** the president could dismiss the prime minister and dissolve the legislature —which he did in 1988. Consequently, after Zia's death in a plane crash the same year, the country was left without a president, prime minister or assemblies. **Ghulam Ishaq Khan,** the chairman of the senate and next in line, became Interim President. Elections were held as planned resulting in a contest between **Mian Nawaz Sharif,** whose program resembled that of late **Zia ul-Haq** and the victor, Z.A. Bhutto's daughter, **Benazir Bhutto,** who ran on her father's **Pakistan People's Party** platform

BENAZIR BHUTTO —Prime Minister (1988-1990 and 1993-1997)
Benazir Bhutto's accession in 1988 signaled the end of repressive dictatorial rule and the welcome return of democracy. Her popularity and productivity suffered, however, as her vendetta against **Mian Muhammed Nawaz Sharif,** a close ally of Zia—her father's killer— spiraled out of control.

Bhutto saw Nawaz Sharif, who had been elected Chief Minister of the Punjab, as a potent rival who needed to be destroyed before he could destroy her. The rivalry brought the government to a standstill.

Bhutto's popularity was also hurt by her husband, whose practice of pocketing money after every big business transaction that needed governmental approval earned him the moniker of "**Mr. 10%.**" Bhutto's husband, Asif Ali Zardan remains in jail in Pakistan on corruption charges.

MIAN MUHAMMED NAWAZ SHARIF —Prime Minister (1990-1993 and 1997-1999)
With Bhutto's ineffective administration and the rise in anti-PPP sentiment, Nawaz Sharif rose to power and won the 1990 elections. Like his predecessor **Zia ul-Haq,** Sharif tried to "wrap himself in Islam," winning the approval of religious fundamentalists. He also championed the cause of the industrial-commercial class that had long been in the shadow of the country's agrarian elite. The prime minister had a powerful hold over all the country's major institutions apart from the army.

Ms. Bhutto beat him at the polls again in 1993, but Sharif recaptured his position in 1997. Two years later, he was deposed in a military coup.

PERVEZ MUSHARRAF—Chief Executive (1999-2001), President (2001-present)
Sharif's downfall was the result of a disagreement between the prime minister and his chief of army staff, **General Pervez Musharraf,** over military tactics in **Kargil,** Kashmir. The military seized power when Sharif report-

edly prevented a plane carrying Musharraf from landing in Karachi. After the aircraft finally set down, the prime minister was deposed and, on October 12, 1999, Musharraf declared himself Chief Executive. Sharif was later charged with treason and hijacking a commercial airline and was sentenced to life in prison. His sentenced was commuted in 200 to exile in Saudi Arabia.

Musharraf also dismissed the standing president, **Rafiq Tarar**, dissolved the national and provisional assemblies and suspended the constitution (it was restored in December 2002 with changes). In June 2001, he appointed himself President of Pakistan and legitimized his rule in a referendum held on April 30, 2002. As a result of the referendum, Musharraf's term as president was extended to 2007.

In November, 2002, Musharraf agreed to hand over certain powers to a newly elected parliament and agreed to share some of his authority with a prime minister (**Mir Zafarullah Khan Jamali**, elected October 2002, stepped down July 2004). Musharraf, who continued to serve as the Head of State, also promised to leave his post in the military by December 31, 2004.

Musharraf worked closely with American President George W. Bush in the "war on terror" and helped defeat the Taliban by cutting off supply lines, providing logistical support and supplying vital intelligence. His cooperation with the American president, however, caused the consternation of some militant constituents who berated him for "complying to [sic] the wicked Bush's orders" and made a number of attempts on his life.

Musharraf's support for the U.S. stopped short of the Iraq war, however, and he refused to send any Pakistan troops to the Middle East nation without a UN resolution.

PRIME MINISTER

Under Pakistan's constitution, the prime minister is the leader of the party in the National Assembly with the most popular votes. The President has the constitutional power to remove the prime minister by dissolving the National Assembly triggering new elections.

After the coup d'etat of Perez Musharraf, the office of prime minister was suspended while Musharraf acted as both the President and Prime Minister. General elections were held again in October 2002 with no party gaining the majority.

ZAFARULLAH KHAN JAMALI

After weeks of negotiations and political wrangling **Zafarullah Khan Jamali** from the pro-Musharraf **PML-Q** party was appointed Prime Minister of Pakistan. In his 19-month tenure, the unpopular prime minister was dogged by accusations of nepotism and ineffectiveness. He resigned in June 2004 handing over the post to a caretaker prime minister, president of the PML-Q, **Chaudhry Shujaat Hussain**.

SHAUKAT AZIZ

Chaudhry Shujaat Hussain acted as prime minister until his intended successor had won a seat in the Parliament. As was planned, Hussain resigned in August, 2004 allowing Shaukat Aziz, Pakistan's finance minister and close confidant of Musharraf, to assume the position.

GOVERNORS GENERAL
Mohammad Ali Jinnah (ML, Muslim League) 1947- 1948
Khwaja Nazimuddin (ML) 1948-1951
Ghulam Mohammad (ML) 1951-1955
Iskander Ali Mirza (military) 1955-1956

PRESIDENTS
Iskander Ali Mirza (RP, Republican Party) 1956-1958
Mohammad Ayub Khan (military) 1969-1971
Zulfikar Ali Bhutto (PPP, Pakistan People's Party) 1971-1973
Fazal Elahi Chaudhry (PPP) 1973-1978
Mohammad Zia ul-Haq (military) 1978-1988
Ghulam Ishaq Khan (no party) 1988-1993
Wasim Sajjad (PML-N, Pakistan Muslim League, Nawaz Sharif Faction) 1993
Mohammad Rafiq Tarar (PML-N) 1988-2001
Pervez Musharraf (military) 2001-

PRIME MINISTERS
Nawabzada Liaquat Ali Khan (ML) 1947-1951
Khwaja Nazimuddin (ML) 1951-1953
Mohammad Ali Bogra (ML) 1953-1955
Chauhdry Mohammad Ali (ML) 1955-1956
Hussain Shaheed Suhrawardy (AL, Awami League) 1956-1957
Malik Firooz Khan Noon (RP) 1957-1958
Mohammad Ayub Khan (military) 1958-1969
Agha Mohammad Yahya Khan (military) 1969-1971
Nurul Amin (PPP) 1971
Zulfikar Ali Bhutto (PPP) 1971-1977
Mohammad Zia ul-Haq (military) 1977-1985
Mohammad Khan Junejo (PML) 1985-1988
Mohammad Zia ul-Haq (military) 1988-1988
Benazir Bhutto (PPP) 1988-1990
Ghulam Mustapha Jatoi (NPP, National People's Party) 1990
Mian Mohammad Nawaz Sharif (PML-N) 1990-1993
Balakh Sher Mazari (PML-N) 1993
Mian Mohammad Nawaz Sharif (PML-N) 1993
Moeen Qureshi (no party) 1993
Benazir Bhutto (PPP) 1993-1996
Malik Miraj Khalid (no party) 1996-1997
Mian Mohammad Nawaz Sharif 1997-1999
Pervez Musharraf (military) 1999-2002
Mir Zafarullah Khan Jamali (PML-Q, Pakistan Muslim League –Quaid-i-Azam faction) 2002-2004
Chaudhry Shujaat Hussain (PML-Q) 2004
Shaukat Aziz (PML-Q) 2004-

BANGLADESH

When **Dr. Allama Mohammed Iqbal** first proposed a separate state for Indian Muslims in 1930, he did not include the area of Bengal. Nor did **Rehmat Ali** include an initial for the territory in his acronym "P.A.K.I.S.T.A.N." But by the time Ali Jinnah's conception of a Muslim state independent from India was ratified on paper, first in the **Lahore Resolution** in 1940 and then the **Delhi Resolution** in 1946, the new state of "Pakistan" incorporated all areas of India with a Muslim majority, including Bengal.

Despite being separated by 1,000 miles of foreign territory (India), the two wings of Pakistan shared a common bond—Islam. Linguistically, culturally and economically, though, "West Pakistan" and "East Pakistan" were very different. The more homogeneous Bengalis spoke Bangla, a language related to Sanskrit, for example, while West Pakistanis spoke a number of different languages and were ethnically more diverse.

No small minority, the Bengalis were also greater in number than the people living in all the provinces of Western Pakistan combined. Consequently, more people spoke Bangla in the new country (more than 50% of the population) than any other language. Urdu, by comparison, was only spoken by 3% of the population, and mostly the upper classes at that. But since Urdu was closer to Arabic and Persian and hence more "Islamic" than Bangla, according to the Urdu-speaking leaders of the Muslim League, Urdu was adopted as the national language.

Numerical advantage also didn't guarantee the Bengalis equivalent representation in the national government. Most upper-class Muslim immigrants from India – *Mohajirs* who had served in the British administration before independence – had migrated to the western wing of Pakistan, where they set up and dominated the country's government. The imbalance allowed the central government (based in Karachi, West Pakistan) to legislate in favor of the West—for instance by collecting money earned from East Bengali exports to finance development in the capital and by levying taxes to invest in the Punjab-dominated military.

In June 1949, a group of dissatisfied Bengalis formed the country's first opposition party, the **Awami League**. The party sought to confine the role of the central government to issues of defense and foreign affairs. It also asked for separate foreign trade agreements for both East and West Pakistan, a separate paramilitary force in East Bengal, separate currencies and the right for Bengalis to levy taxes and collect revenue.

21

Under the regime of **Ayub Khan**, Bengali nationalist politics became particularly militant. Khan's administration had placed Awami League President **Mujibur Rehman** under detention for his purported involvement in a conspiracy to separate East Bengal from Pakistan with India's help. The mass uprisings that followed forced Ayub Khan to resign and to hand over power to military chief **Yahya Khan** in 1969.

To pacify East Pakistan, Yahya Khan promised that seats won in future elections would be distributed according to population size. East Bengal would receive the majority of the seats, 169; Punjab would receive 85 seats; Sindh, 28; NWFP, 19; Balochistan, 5; and the Tribal Areas, 7.

When the **Awami League** won 167 of 313 possible seats in Pakistan's national government, it had clearly outnumbered the opposition. **Zulfikar Ali Bhutto's Pakistan People's Party (PPP)** representing West Pakistani bourgeoisie had won only 88 seats. The threat of East Pakistan dominance in the government and its potential role in framing Pakistan's new constitution was more than Bhutto, the military bureaucracy, and business community—all West Pakistan-dominated—were willing to accept.

While negotiations were taking place between the Yahya administration, the Awami League and the PPP (which eventually boycotted the session) troops were sent to East Pakistan to suppress Bengali nationalism. The Awami League's refusal to compromise by softening its autonomous demands prompted Yahya to dissolve the civilian cabinet.

Violent military clashes in Bengal resulted in the deaths of many civilians and turned the quest for political self-rule into national struggle. Political leaders of the **Awami League** set up their own government-in-exile in India where they proclaimed the independence of Bangladesh from Pakistan and declared war on their former partners. Supported by India, the Bengalis were able to force Pakistan's surrender in December 1971 and form an independent government the next year. With **Z. A. Bhutto** at the helm of the new government, a demoralized and truncated Pakistan finally recognized "Bangladesh" in 1974.

PROVINCES AT A GLANCE

Main Provinces	Capital	Ethnicity
Punjab	Lahore	Punjabi
Balochistan	Quetta	Balochi, Pushtu, Brahui
North West Frontier	Peshawar	Pushtu, Hindko, Kashmiri
Province		Khowar Kohistani, Gujar
		Kalashin
Sindh	Karachi	Sindhi and Seraiki

Other Territories
      Federally Administered Tribal Areas
      Islamabad Capital Territory
      Pakistan-administered portion of disputed Jammu and Kashmir
      region - (Azad Kashmir and the Northern Areas.)

PUNJAB

In addition to being the wealthiest and most influential province in Pakistan dominating political and business life, Punjab is also the most ethnically and culturally homogenous. Most Punjabis are descendants of the Aryans who occupied the area in the 15th to 12th centuries B.C. and they identify themselves in terms of their *quam*, a tribal affiliation based on lineage and occupation.

Before the British-imposed **Radcliffe Line** divided Punjab in 1947 between India and Pakistan, the land had been shared by Muslims (55%), Hindus (30%) and Sikhs. The Partition resulted in a mass migration of millions of people across the new borders and the deaths of about a million others. Sikhs and Hindus fled to the Indian side of Punjab while the Punjabi Muslims settled in Pakistan's section becoming the country's most populous ethnic group after the Bengalis. Punjabi dominance in the Pakistan military and government created resentment in other provinces, especially in East Pakistan (now Bangladesh), as did the concentration of wealth in Punjab.

Punjab, whose name derives from the words *panj*, meaning five, and *ab*, meaning waters, lies at the source of five major Indus River tributaries. Before the British established an expansive irrigation system, the region was plagued by floods near the water sources and barren land elsewhere. Punjab has since become the nation's most fertile province as well as its leader in industrial development.

SINDH

To the Aryans, who lived in the Indus River area about 1700 B.C., the size of the river that flowed through Sindh to the Arabian Sea was so great that they called it an "ocean," or "Sindhu," in Sanskrit. The name became "Indus" in Greek (giving India its name) "Sintow" in Chinese and "Hindu" to the Persians – who call the area "Hindustan." Pakistan's province of "Sindh," with its natural harbor at the mouth of the Indus River, has had a rich history from that time on.

In A.D. 711, **Mohammed bin Qasim** built the country's first mosque at the Sindhi port city of Banbhore. From there he introduced Islam to the subcontinent and the religion flourished after the arrival of the Sufis some time later.

When the Indus River changed course, the city of **Karachi** replaced Banbhore as Sindh's significant seaport and was transformed from a small fishing village into one of the most developed cities in India by the British after they annexed Sindh in 1843.

Highways, railroads, irrigation canals and a number of new businesses (most run by Sindhi Hindus) were established to service British military personnel and vessels heading to Afghanistan. Outside the urban areas, however, traditional life changed very little. A rigid feudal system separated society into *waderas*, or landlords (many of them Balochi in origin) and *haris*, or rural farm workers.

After Partition, the urban face of Sindh changed considerably. Most members of the Hindu middle class elite, who had dominated business activity under the British, fled the area along with their Hindu brethren. In their place, a new group of non-Sindhi Muslims from India (*Mohajirs*) moved in and took over many of the vacated businesses. When **Ali Jinnah** named Karachi Pakistan's new capital and turned the city into a separate "federal district" within Sindh, many of the educated Urdu-speaking *Mohajirs* also assumed lofty positions in the country's government.

The locals vociferously objected to the non-Sindhi refugees taking over jobs that they believed should have gone to the "sons of the soil." As more positions were filled with Urdu-speakers and the use of the local Sindhi language was discouraged in places like Karachi University, incidents of discrimination worsened.

Moreover, with the 1971 arrival of Urdu-speaking Muslims from Bangladesh (*Biharis*), the influx of Afghan Pathan refugees in the 1980s and the steady flow of Punjabi immigrants looking for work, the Sindhis had become minorities in their own towns.

Only **Z.A. Bhutto**, himself a Sindhi *wadera*, championed the Sindhi cause by courting the lieutenants of **Ghulam Murtaza Shah Sayed (G. M. Sayed)** whose followers advocated a sovereign and independent "Sindhu Desh" ("Sindhi homeland").[1]

The *Mohajirs* rose up violently in response. From that time on, the local Sindhis were great supporters of Bhutto, his allies and his successors and vehemently rebelled against the regime of Bhutto's usurper and executioner, **Zia ul-Haq**.

In the 1980s, Sindhis campaigned against Zia's extralegal accession to power and demanded the return to free elections. In retaliation, Zia brutally put down the Sindhi insurrectionists in a military assault that left more than 1000 people dead.

For their own protection, the *Mohajirs* organized themselves into a powerful political party, the **Mohajir Qaumi Movement** (MQM, later renamed the Mutahi Qaumi Movement).

[1] At the time, a bill was passed by the Sindh Assembly (where the PPP had a majority headed by the Chief Minister) reestablishing the local Sindhi language as the state language in place of Urdu.

NORTHWEST FRONTIER PROVINCE

Long before the British created the "North West Frontier Province," the culturally rich area in the north of the province from the Khyber Pass to the Indus River was called **Gandhara** by tribes living there in the 2nd millennium B.C.

Gandhara served as a gateway to Central Asia during the sovereignty of many great dynasties form the Persian **Achaemenids** in the 6th century B.C. to the **Mauryans, Bactrians, Parthians** and finally the **Kushans**—who cultivated one of the greatest Buddhist civilizations in the area in the 1st century A.D. The Khyber Pass, which cut through the Suleiman mountain ranges, allowed traders and pilgrims to spread their cultures and religions to Asia through Gandhara from the Middle East and Europe and back again along the famous **Silk Road**.

The glory of Gandhara waned, however, after a string of invasions by Sassanian Persians, Huns, Turks, Moghuls, Afghans, Sikhs and others. By the 12th century A.D., the name "Gandhara" had disappeared from use.

The **Moghuls**, who had traveled through the Khyber Pass in 1505, ruled the area for two centuries until insurrections by the native Pathan tribesmen compelled them to cede the area to the Persian **Nadir Shah** of the Afghan **Durrani** dynasty. In 1799, the Durranis gave Lahore to the Sikhs, whose empire— stretching from Punjab to Kashmir—was valued as a strategic buffer state between British India and the Russians, who appeared to be encroaching form the northwest through Afghanistan.

After Sikh leader **Ranjit Sikh** died in 1840, the British attempted to fortify their northwest frontier by sending forces to the area and installing a puppet regime in Afghanistan. After two unsuccessful wars fought against Afghanistan, however, the British decided to negotiate the creation of a boundary line between British India and Afghanistan.

The placement of this boundary in 1893, called the **Durand Line**, gave the British a strategic advantage by keeping all the high mountain ranges on the British side of the territory, but it ignored existing tribal associations. The line was drawn right through Pathan tribal territory.

The colonists were never able to subdue the fiercely independent Pathans. Therefore, like the Persians, Kushans, Huns and Moghuls before them (and the Pakistanis after them), the British offered some of the aristocratic Pathans important posts in the military and bureaucracy and let the rest govern themselves.

After Partition, the frontier tribes voted to join Pakistan.

PATHANS (PASHTUNS)

The Pathans believe their 15-million strong family of "relatives" is descended from a common ancestor named **Qais**. It is believed that Qais was given the name **P'thun** (the source of the word Pathan) by the prophet Mohammed, whom he met in Medina in the 7th century. Among Qais' many children was a son called **Afghana,** who lived with his four sons in Afghanistan ("Afghana's country"). When Afghana's sons left to seek their fortunes, they headed in four different directions: towards Lahore, Multan, Quetta and the NWFP areas of Dir, Swat and Hazara. Each contemporary tribe takes its name from one of the founding fathers and shares a deep kinship with other tribe members.

The North West Frontier Province (NWFP) is divided into two sections: the "settled areas" inhabited primarily by Pathan farmers, and the "tribal regions," an autonomous area along the border with Afghanistan governed by tribal law under the supervision of the Pakistan government. Unlike their agricultural counterparts, the Pathans living in the "tribal regions" make their livings as shepherds, smugglers or arms makers and strictly observe the tribal code of behavior called "*Pushtunwali.*"

Pushtunwali is based on four main principles: hospitality, revenge, submission (to a victor) and honor. A guest in a Pathan's home, for instance, is treated with the utmost hospitality, even if the guest is an enemy. Also according to the code, the murder or assault of a family or tribe member must be avenged with the death of an equivalent member of the killer's family – a practice that has kept tribes feuding for generations.

Observance of the *pushtunwali* code is monitored by the tribal elders (*kasha*), tribal leaders (*malik*), and religious leaders (*mullahs*), who may debate issues in a general assembly (*loya jirga*). If necessary, a temporary militia (*lashkar*) may be summoned to keep order.

Afghanistan and Pashtunistan

When **Ahmed Shah Durrani** founded Afghanistan in 1747, it was perceived to be a Pathan tribal confederacy designed to defend Pathan interests in the face of non-Pathan rivals. But as Afghanistan extended its borders north into Russia at the encouragement of the British—who hoped to develop Afghanistan as a buffer state—the Afghans incorporated vast areas made up of minority ethnic groups. A sense of diminished distinction and the loss of territory to the British on the Indian side of the **Durand Line** led the Pathans of Afghanistan to try to reestablish some form of political unity with the Pathans over the border.

Pathans on the Indian side of the Line, meanwhile, were angry over Britain's role in the division of their territory and the economic disparity they had created between the wealthy *khans*, who were allied with the British, and the rest of the peasant and artisan population.

At the time of Partition in 1947, Pathan **Ghaffar Khan** and his son, **Wali Khan**, played on these grievances to demand an independent "**Pashtunistan**," or "land of the Pashtuns (Pathans)," either to be formed as a provincial autonomous region within Pakistan or a separate country. Although the Pathans agreed to join Pakistan and Wali Khan and his father were put in prison, the dream of "Pashtunistan" continued to inspire Pathans.

Pakistan has tried to maintain good relations with the leaders of Afghanistan and has eagerly attempted to repatriate thousands of Afghan Pathan refugees or relocate them to other parts of Pakistan.

BALOCHISTAN

Balochistan, bordered by Afghanistan in the north and Iran in the west, is by far the largest province of Pakistan (42% of the total area) although its population makes up less than 5% of the national total.

More than half of Balochistan's inhabitants live within a small radius of the province's capital, Quetta, its only contemporary city. The rest of the territory is occupied by semi-nomadic **Balochi** and **Brahui** tribespeople, as well as a growing number of Pathans in the north.

The Balochi tribes came to the area from Iran or Syria between the 6th and 14th centuries, subjugating the already settled Brahuis and Meds, and giving the region its name. Until that time, the territory had fallen under a succession of invaders, from the Persians in the 6th century B.C. to the Mughals two millennia later. After the Brahuis reestablished power under **Mir Nasir Khan I** of Kalat in the 18th century, Balochistan came close to being an independent country.

The British became interested in Balochistan as a corridor into Afghanistan during the first **Anglo-Afghan** war in the 1840s and later considered expanding British influence into the area in order to counter Russian expansionism from the northwest. **Sir Robert Sandeman**, the Deputy Commissioner appointed to the region, orchestrated the territory's inclusion into the British Empire in 1887 by cultivating good relations with powerful Baluch and Brahui tribal chiefs (*sardars*) and working within the existing framework of the administration.

At the time of Pakistan's independence in 1947, the last ruler of Kalat (the stronghold of the Khans) cited Britain's promises of Balochi sovereignty to contest the province's incorporation into the new Muslim state. He was ultimately forced to sign the necessary merger documents in 1948, but the drive for Balochistan's self-government continued.

Most of the *sardars* gave up their official administrative powers soon after Pakistan's independence from Britain but retained considerable control over local residents as feudal lords governing by tribal custom. This practice was aggressively challenged by Pakistan's ruling parties after Bangladesh's split from Pakistan in 1971.

With Bangladesh's independence, moreover, all insurgent movements were viewed as serious threats to Pakistan's integrity. Although Balochi guerrillas had been waging nationalistic struggles from the time of Britain's withdrawal from the sub-continent, they were severely repressed after 1971.

In defiance against the Pakistan government, Balochis refused to implement various federal measures and continued to demand regional autonomy and a restructured central government. To quash the potential revolt, **Zulfikar Ali Bhutto** sent Pakistani troops backed by Iranian forces to suppress the rebels. Thousands of Balochi guerrillas and Pakistani soldiers died in confrontations that took place between 1973 and 1977 leaving a legacy of hatred, strong separatist tendencies and a politicized population that felt alienated form the central government.

The uprisings in Balochistan, like the war in Bangladesh, further demonstrated that Islam alone could not bond the disparate groups living in Pakistan. It also proved that the central government could not completely override local tribal loyalties.

Major Ethnic Groups in Pakistan

Map based on Selig S. Harisson, <u>In Afghanistan's Shadow: Baluch Nationalism and Soviet Temptations</u> (New York: Carnegie Endowment for International Peace, 1981) p. 84

KASHMIR AT A GLANCE

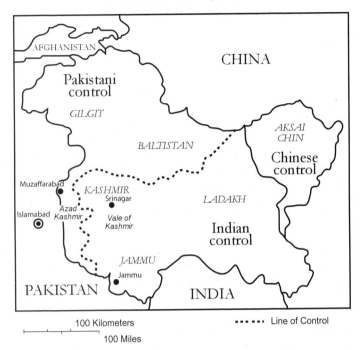

100 Kilometers

100 Miles

••••• Line of Control

KASHMIR

At the northern tip of India, the northeastern part of Pakistan and the western edge of China lies a piece of territory whose ownership has been violently disputed for half a century. Collectively known simply as "Kashmir" by much of the world, the divided land has destroyed diplomatic relations between India and Pakistan, drained both countries of badly needed capital, and distressed the international community over the potentially devastating consequences of war between the nuclear-armed rivals.

GEOGRAPHY

Although the contentious area is popularly called "Kashmir" or "Jammu and Kashmir," after the most populous sections, the state is actually an amalgam of five regions that were united by **Gulab Singh** in the 19th century.

The largest region, **Ladakh**, nicknamed "little Tibet" because of its strong cultural ties with its East Asian neighbor Tibet and its predominantly Buddhist population, was once situated along the historical **Silk Road** trade route. Today it is divided between China, which occupies a portion called **Aksai Chin**, and India.

Jammu in the southwest is overwhelmingly Hindu with a Muslim minority. Most of the region lies within the Indian-held side of the state. The rest of Azad (Free) Jammu is held by Pakistan.

The Kashmir valley (or Vale of Kashmir) is home to more than half of the state's seven million people. Most native Kashmiris practice a centuries-old Sufi form of Islam and maintain a unique multi-cultural identity called "**Kashmiriyat**." The rest of the population is made up of a significant number of Hindu minorities called **Pandits** and a smaller number of Sikhs.

After 1949, the Kashmir Valley was split into two parts along the "**Line of Control**." The northern section temporarily became part of Pakistan as "**Azad Kashmir**" and the south became a part of India. The area of "Azad Jammu and Kashmir" is treated much like a legitimate province with its own legislative assembly and high court in AJ & K's capital, **Muzaffarabad**.

KASHMIR BACKGROUND

After incorporating the area of Jammu and Kashmir into his empire in the **Siege of Multan** in 1819, the Sikh leader, **Maharaja** (Prince) **Ranjit Singh**, granted Jammu to one of his leaders, Maharajah **Gulab Singh**, a Hindu, to reward him for his service.

When the British conquered the Sikhs in the wars of 1846, Gulab Singh was again rewarded, this time for supporting the British against the Sikhs. Through the **Treaty of Amritsar**, the British sold the Hindu Maharaja the predominantly Muslim area of Kashmir and Ladakh. Thus Gulab Singh had integrated Jammu, Kashmir and the Ladakh regions into one administrative unit ruled by his descendents until the middle of the 20th century.

At the time of independence in 1947, however, all princes within the British Empire were instructed to join their princely states with either the new Muslim state of Pakistan, or remain within a truncated India. While most of the princes quickly considered the proximity of their principality to the two countries and the wishes of their constituents when making their decisions, **Maharaja Hari Singh** of Kashmir hesitated. The Hindu prince, at the head of a mainly Muslim region, understood that if he joined Pakistan, he would have to abdicate his throne. Joining India, on the other hand, would betray the wishes of the people.

Pathan tribesmen, meanwhile, feared that Hari Singh was planning to collaborate with India. To save their Muslim brothers, the Pathans marched into Kashmir forcing the Maharajah to turn to the Indians for military protection. Pakistan immediately responded to India's retaliatory advance on the Pathan warriors, plunging the two countries into their first war over Kashmir in 1947.

Two years later, a UN cease-fire agreement was signed assigning the two countries a piece of territory on each side of the **Line of Control** to administer until a popular vote (plebiscite) would determine a permanent resolution. Gilgit, Baltistan and the western portion of the Vale of Kashmir were granted to Pakistan while Jammu, Ladakh and East Kashmir went to India.

PAKISTAN PERSPECTIVE

According to Pakistan, **Hari Singh** was pressured into acceding Kashmir to India in violation of the Rules of Partition and against the wishes of the Kashmir people who wanted independence. The locals, moreover, had risen up against the Maharajah, forced him to flee from Srinigar and had formed their own government. But the Indians ignored their sovereignty by invading the country and dismantling the last legal representation of the people. By refusing to hold the promised plebiscite, Pakistanis claim, the Indians continued to violate the cease-fire agreement.

INDIAN PERSPECTIVE

The Indians, on the other hand, believe that Hari Singh's decision to join India was perfectly legal and that it was the Pakistanis who had invaded Indian Territory and pressured the Kashmiris to rise up. For the last decade, they further claim, religious extremists from around the world have been infiltrating the territory and turning the locals away from their tolerant and pacifist Kashmiriyat ways leading them to joint the militant "brotherhood of Islam."

The Pakistan government, they say, even trained and armed radicals to fight in Kahsmir and terrorize India on behalf of the Kashmiris for Pakistan's political benefit. Islamabad has denied these allegations claiming the militants acted on their own with the assent and help of the indigenous population.

As for the plebiscite question, Indians maintain that elections previously held on their territory demonstrated that the people living in India's side of Kashmir wanted to remain part of the democratic, tolerant and secular Indian union and that a popular vote was unnecessary.

People living in the Pakistan-occupied parts of the area, they contend, haven't had the opportunity to learn what democracy is all about and live in fear of being killed if they dare to speak out against the country.

KAHSMIR AN INDEPENDENT COUNTRY?

While India and Pakistan fought over claims to the territory of Jammu and Kashmir, members of the local population were seeking self-determination and the preservation of the Kashmiri identity.

Kashmir's first political party was formed in the wake of Muslim protests against Hindu Maharajah **Hari Singh's** rule in the 1930s, by **Sheikh Mohammed Abdullah**. The **All Jammu and Kashmir Muslim Conference**, which became the secular **National Conference (NC)** in 1939, championed the cause of the poor rural Muslims and lower-caste Hindus against the wealthy landed gentry. For a few days in 1949 between Singh's departure and India's entry in the war against Pakistan, the NC took over *de facto* administration of Kashmir. Sheikh Abdullah also served as Chief Minister on the Indian side of the **Line of Control** after the 1949 cease-fire agreement. Under India's Constitution adopted the same year, the State of Kashmir was to enjoy a special status of autonomy until the plebiscite was held to let Kashmiris decide their destiny.

With the enactment of the **Delhi Agreement** in 1952, however, self-determination was supplanted by Kashmir's official incorporation into India's union. Moreover, Sheikh Abdullah, whose party had won all the seats in the state election of 1951, was dismissed and incarcerated because of questions about his loyalty to India, and was in and out of prison for the next 20 years.

Although the India state of Jammu and Kashmir was granted more autonomy than other Indian states (for example, it was allowed to fly its own flag and elect its own governors with New Delhi's approval), the local government was nonetheless weak, and civil unrest and repression were rampant.

In this atmosphere, both the Pakistanis and Indians attempted to influence the local population by highlighting their religious differences. India supported the Hindus and Pakistan appealed to the Muslims, including members of the **Jammu Kashmir Liberation Front** (JKLF), a group formed in 1977, to push for Kashmir's inherent right to self-determination, urging them to join in a fight for independence and ultimately incorporation into the respective countries.

The tolerant multi-ethnic **Kashmiriyat** identity was lost to externally motivated political agendas.

WHY KASHMIR MATTERS TO INDIA
Unlike the British, who treated Kashmir simply as a frontier post, the Indians see Kashmir as the first line of defense against incursion from the Chinese or Pakistanis from the north. The loss of Kashmir, they believe, would leave India's capital, New Delhi, and the entire northern region of India vulnerable to attack.

At the same time, the area is seen as an integral part of India and any suggestion of abandoning the fight to keep it within the nation would be viewed as a betrayal of India's national identity and concession to the Islamic militants.

WHY KASHMIR MATTERS TO PAKISTAN

When the **Line of Control** was drawn, it left the headwaters of the Indus and other rivers—essential for Pakistan's agricultural economy—in Indian territory. Although the water problem was settled a decade later with an irrigation treaty, the area is still considered vitally important for the future of the nation.

The issue of Kashmir has become emotional glue that has bound the otherwise fractious population of Pakistan by rallying the people around a common cause. Almost every Pakistan leader has used Kashmir to consolidate his or her position.

WHY KASHMIR MATTERS TO THE WORLD

With the advent of nuclear capabilities in Pakistan and India, the rest of the world has become particularly concerned about the lack of stability in the region. When altercations arise, as they did when terrorists from militant Kashmir parities attacked India's parliament building in December 2001, the international community has been eager to mediate. Even on the subjects of international interference, though, the Pakistanis and Indians differ. While Islamabad welcomes third party intervention, Delhi condemns outside help as a violation of the **Simla Accord**.

Kashmir has also been a popular destination for militants, including some Al Qaeda terrorists fleeing Afghanistan and parts of Pakistan.

Economically, the standoff in Kashmir has drained both countries of money that could have been used to develop healthy financial infrastructures and has prevented the countries from collaborating on potentially lucrative projects like the proposed oil and gas pipeline to be built from Iran to India through Pakistan. The looming specter of war has also scared off potential foreign investors who would prefer to spend their money in stable countries with strong economies.

KASHMIR TIMELINE

1925 – **Maharaja Hari Singh** ascends throne of Kashmir

1932 – **Sheikh Abdullah** becomes **Muslim Conference** (NC) president

1947 – Local revolt repressed by Maharaja Hari Singh. NWFP Pathans join revolt. Hari Singh asks for help from India. Accedes to India. Indian troops arrive and fight. Pakistan and India fight over Kashmir.

1948 – Sheik Abdullah becomes Prime Minister of Kashmir.

1949 – UN cease-fire, call for plebiscite imposed. Hari Singh leaves Kashmir for good.

1951 – Abdullah wins first post-independence elections.

1953 – Abdullah is dismissed as Prime Minister and arrested by India.

1954 – Kashmir's Constituent Assembly ratifies accession to India.

1958 – China attacks India

1962 – Talks between India and Pakistan over Kashmir

1965 – Pakistan attacks India, hoping for local revolt. This war is known as "**Operation Gibraltar.**"

1971 – Bangladesh war, **Cease-fire Line** becomes **Line of Control**

1972 – **Simla Accord**

1977 – **Jammu and Kashmir Liberation Front** (JKLF) formed in Britain.

1979 – USSR invades Afghanistan

1981 – Sheikh Abdullah's son, **Farooq Abdullah**, takes over office.

1990 – Kashmiris demand implementation of Plebiscite. 140,000 Hindus leave Kashmir for refugee camps in Jammu.

1998 – India and Pakistan perform nuclear tests

1999 – India and Pakistan clash militarily over **Kargil**.

2001 – 3000 conflict-related deaths occurred. Human rights violations are widespread and endemic.
December – **Prevention of Terrorism Bill** is passed in Indian Parliament
December 12 – Attack on Indian parliament believed to have been ordered by Pakistani militants.
December – Threat of war escalates

2002 – Pakistan arrests some militants. India demands more arrests.

2002 – India and Pakistan on brink of war.

2003 -- Both India and Pakistan test missiles.
Musharraf and Vajpayee make gestures toward peace.
India and Pakistan agree to reopen a cross-border rail service.

2004 -- The leaders of India and Pakistan, Atal Behari Vajpayee and Pervez Musharraf, meet for the first time since 2002.

FOREIGN RELATIONS

AFGHANISTAN

Afghanistan and Pakistan share a history that goes back thousands of years from joint incorporation into Cyrus the Great's **Achaemenid Empire** to inclusion in **Ahmed Shah Durrani's** first Afghan kingdom in the 18th century. In fact, many Afghans believed some of Pakistan's land still belongs to Afghanistan because of the large shared **Pathan** (Pashtun) population on both sides of the countries' boundary lines.

The current border was drawn in 1839 by **Sir Mortimer Durand**, a British bureaucrat who hoped to strengthen the status of Afghanistan as a buffer state between then-British colony of India and the expanding Russian Empire. The 19th century "**Durand Line**" served Britain strategically by incorporating all the mountain cliffs on the Indian side but ignored ethnic and cultural realities when it was drawn right through Pathan tribal territory. Although the reigning Afghan King, **Abdul Rahman Khan** had accepted the designated border for a term of 100 years, the division was never certified by a legislative body, leading some Afghans to claim that the "imaginary line" was never valid.

When Pakistan was liberated from India in 1947 and the "Indian" territories were being divided, Afghanistan tried to insist that the people living in Pashtun tribal areas be given the opportunity to join Pakistan or Afghanistan or incorporate into a new state of "**Pashtunistan**," ("land of the Pashtuns"). Instead, like the rest of the subcontinent, the Pashtuns had to choose between joining India or Pakistan with no option for independence. Afghanistan twice severed diplomatic relations with Pakistan over this issue.

In 1973, **Sardar Daud**, who had come to power in Afghanistan by staging a coup against his cousin, **King Zahir Shah**, actively promoted the idea of an independent "Pashtunistan" provoking Pakistan Prime Minister Z.A. Bhutto, and later President Zia ul-Haq, into establishing diplomatic relations with the new Afghan ruler.

When Sardar Daud and his family members were murdered in a bloody Marxist coup five years later, the "Pashtunistan question" took a back seat to the new threat of a Soviet invasion.

SOVIET-AFGHAN WAR, 1979

In December 1979, the Soviets installed **Babrak Karmal** to head the new Afghan government and Chief of Army Staff Zia saw an opportunity to strengthen Pakistan's international image and legitimize his own regime by heading the resistance movement.

In and around Peshawar, Pakistan trained and supplied seven parties of pro-Pakistan Afghan *mujahideen* or "holy warriors," to fight the Soviets. The

Zia regime hoped that claims to Pakistan's land would end forever once the Pakistan-friendly Pathan resistance fighters came to power in Kabul. With their allies in place, furthermore, Pakistan could enjoy "**strategic depth**" (see People and Policies) against its enemy, India.

The US, in the middle of its own Cold War against the USSR, saw Pakistan as a valuable bulwark against their communist foes and supplied massive amounts of military aid and supplies to the country to help fight the war in Afghanistan. The aid was then funneled though Peshawar to the *mujahideen*.

The call to *jihad* (holy war) against the Soviet "infidel" intruders was answered by Muslims around the world who felt it was their Islamic duty to rescue Afghanistan from the non-believers. Turkey, Saudi Arabia, the United Arab Emirates and Egypt all sent fighters and recognized Zia ul-Haq as a "warrior for Islam."

Pakistan enjoyed unprecedented international prestige and financial aid at this time although it also suffered some consequences. Hundreds of thousands of Afghan refugees flooded the country needing shelter, food and relief. The influx of weapons and drugs (from opium-rich Afghanistan) also precipitated Pakistan's "**Kalashnikov culture**."(see People and Policies). After the Soviets withdrew from Afghanistan, aid from the West was discontinued almost as abruptly as it had been initiated, even though the Soviets continued to shell Pakistan in retaliation.

The *mujahideen* finally captured Kabul in 1992 and overthrew the neo-communist puppet-regime of **Najibullah**. But the victorious *mujahideen* did not come from the well armed, but squabbling, Pathan parties based in Peshawar and supported by Pakistan. Rather, the city fell to the better organized and more united Tajik/Uzbek forces of **Burhanuddin Rabbani Ahmed Shah Massoud**, who was then recognized as Afghanistan's legitimate leader by the United Nations and India.

For the first time in 300 years, Pathans did not control Afghanistan's capital, and the rest of the country was divided into warring fiefdoms run by bellicose warlords.

In desperation, Pakistan, and especially the **ISI** (Inter-Services Intelligence) put all their resources behind **Gulbuddin Hekmatyar**, one of the Peshawar-based *mujahideen* party leaders, in hopes that he could displace the **Rabbani/Massoud** government and unify the country under a pro-Pakistan, Pathan government.

For Pakistan, a friendly and stable regime in Afghanistan was critical for economic, political and strategic reasons. Islamabad was eager to open trade routes through Afghanistan to the Central Asian Republics, and a pacified Afghan Pathan population was necessary to ensure against renewed calls for

Pakistan in a Nutshell

"Pashtunistan" carved out of Pakistan territory.

Moreover, an armed and pliant Afghan regime could provide the country with an important base from which to pursue its objectives in Kashmir.

When the ISI's henchman, **Hekmatyar**, failed to consolidate the country under his rule, newly elected Pakistan Prime Minister **Benazir Bhutto** (in her second term of office, 1993-1996) turned to the **"Taliban"** (students of Islam) to rid Afghanistan of warlords and put an end to the internal strife.

TALIBAN[2]

Most of the original Taliban members were born in Pakistan refugee camps, trained by Pakistani *mujahideen,* and educated at some of Pakistan's most radical religious schools (*madrassas*), such as that of **Maulana Fazlur Rehman** (leader of **Jamiat-e-Ulema Islam**, [JUI]) and **Sami ul-Haq** (who ran the infamous **Haqqania** school, one of Pakistan's largest Islamic schools, a traditional militant training camp).

Since it was believed that the Taliban's interests were religious in nature rather than nationalistic or political, they were considered less likely to push for Pathan solidarity or to ally themselves with any single political party and might even provide an outlet for volatile Islamic radicals living in Pakistan.

Also to **Benazir Bhutto's** advantage, unlike the *mujahideen* of the 1980s, the Taliban were not beholden to the ISI, the intelligence organization that had played a critical role in Bhutto's downfall in her first term of office.

In 1994, the Taliban were employed to help secure trade routes from Pakistan to the Central Asian Republics. By December of that year, they had captured an arms dump and had been joined by more than 10,000 Afghan and Pakistan students.

CONSEQUENCES AND MISSED OPPORTUNITIES

Once in power, however, the Taliban resisted every attempt at control by Islamabad and proved to be more of a detriment to Pakistan than an asset.

The fundamentalist Taliban enforced draconian Islamic codes and punishments, which angered the international community and alienated Taliban supporters. Because of feminist movement in the U.S. protesting against the movement's apparent disregard for human rights, furthermore, an American oil company, **Unocal**, cancelled its plans to build a lucrative pipeline through Afghanistan that would have greatly benefited both Pakistan and Afghanistan.

And rather than easing extremism within Pakistan, the Taliban inspired some religious groups to lash out violently against minority Pakistani Shi'as and the ruling elite. Fundamentalism spread to Pathans on both sides of the bor-

---

[2] For more about the Taliban and Afghanistan, see Roraback, <u>Afghanistan in a Nutshell</u>, Enisen Publishing, 2004

der, creating a new type of Pathan nationalism with a militant Islamic character. Some parts of the country were even beginning to fall victim to trends of "Talibanization."

The Taliban's brand of highly radicalized Islam was also a threat to Russia, which feared the spread of extremism to its southern borders, and to India, which was particularly enraged by a Taliban edict requiring Hindus to identify themselves by wearing yellow badges. Both India and Russia, therefore, actively supported the opposition **Northern Alliance** under **Rabbani**.

By supporting a government that didn't have Pakistan backing, New Delhi also hoped to thwart the Kashmiri militant groups that had been using Afghanistan as a training ground for terrorists planning to conduct guerrilla warfare against India.

WHY PAKISTAN HELPED THE U.S. AGAINST AFGHANISTAN
General Pervez Musharraf found himself caught between a rock and a hard place when the United States requested Islamabad's help to win the "war against terrorism" after the September 11, 2001 airplane attacks on New York City and Washington D.C. Pakistan was being asked to turn its back on the Taliban, a regime it had helped install, as well as the Taliban's guest and financier (and hero to some), **Osama bin Laden**. General Musharraf's acquiescence to American requests upset both sympathetic Pathans and members of the religious right who had risen up against the General in the early stages of the war.

Musharraf, however, felt he had no choice. Pakistan's neighbors had already pledged support to the western allies and—he feared—were using the opportunity to isolate his country by setting up an anti-Pakistan government in Afghanistan.

Had the **Northern Alliance** (renamed the "**United Front**") been installed as the new government rather than the administration of the new Afghan leader, **Hamid Karzai**, Pakistan would have been surrounded on all fronts by nations allied to India. A government run by non-Pathans, moreover, could plunge Afghanistan into another string of civil wars or complete anarchy. If Musharraf didn't participate in the campaign against terrorism, furthermore, the country risked being labeled a terrorist nation itself.

Support for the United States, on the other hand, would win Islamabad international prestige and badly needed financial aid.

"Our critical concerns are our sovereignty, second our economy, third our strategic assets (nuclear and missiles) and fourth our Kashmir cause," explained Musharraf. To appease the religious front, he also pointed out that Pakistan was regarded as a "fort of Islam" and if the "fort" were damaged, Islam would also be damaged.

UNITED STATES

After terrorists crashed airplanes into the World Trade Center in New York City on September 11, 2001, worldwide attention turned to Central Asia, and Pakistan was again courted by the United States to assist in their campaign against Afghanistan. Sanctions placed on Pakistan since 1998 were waived (as they were in India for the sake of parity) and outstanding debts were quickly rescheduled to reward Pakistan for the help the country was expected to provide. In return for economic and military benefits, the Pakistanis were asked to cut off all aid, supplies and transit rights to members of al-Qaeda and the Taliban. They were also urged to share information and allow western forces to stage attacks form Pakistan soil. President Musharraf agreed to these requests and pledged Pakistan's complete support for the U.S. in the fight against terrorism.

But skeptics from both sides were wary of the new relationship. Some Americans believed that it was Pakistan's secret service, the **ISI**, which had been calling the shots in Afghanistan and that Musharraf was powerless. Pakistanis questioned the sincerity of the Americans who had rapidly withdrawn all support form Pakistan after victory was won against the Soviets in Afghanistan in the 1980s.

Fundamentalist Muslims also believed neither **Osama bin Laden** nor Afghanistan was responsible for the terrorist attacks and that the ensuing battle with the poor country was inhumane and unjustified. They also opposed Musharraf's collaboration with the U.S.; a nation that they felt was trying to destroy Islam and was oppressing Muslims by supporting Israel.

In 2002 religious extremists captured and killed Wall Street Journal reporter, **Daniel Pearl**. Although Pearl's captors had demanded the release of Pakistanis captured in Afghanistan and held at the US naval base in Guantanamo Bay, Cuba, Musharraf and others believed they were planning to create a wedge between his regime and the West.

Before the kidnapping, and even before the 2001 terrorist attacks on the US, Musharraf received kudos for his efforts to curb religious extremism in Pakistan. When Pakistan-based militants bombed India's parliament in December 2001, the General quickly responded by banning Kashmiri separatist groups and detaining more than a thousand activists – a move that was met with great approval by the Bush administration. The US especially feared that a confrontation with India would divert attention away from Pakistan's porous border with Afghanistan.

RELIGION

ISLAM[3]

Muhammed, the founder of Islam, was born around A.D. 570 in the city of Mecca into the ruling **Quraysh** tribe. He received the first of his revelations (compiled into the **Quran** [or Koran], Islam's holy book) from **Allah** (God) while meditating in a cave, and he began preaching publicly in A.D. 613. After the Meccans threatened the prophet for challenging their gods and religious practices, Muhammed and his followers fled to Yathrib (**Medina**), where they were offered protection. Muslims call this migration the *hejira*. In Medina, he gathered a tribe of people who accepted him as a prophet and marched back into Mecca, defeating the Quraysh tribe and forcing them to remove all pagan idols and shrines. The new religion of **Islam** (translated as "submission to Allah") soon spread to the rest of Arabia and a century later reached Central Asia.

SHI'ITE(or Shi'a) /SUNNI SPLIT

Muhammed's death in A.D. 632 and his failure to clearly designate a successor led to a division in Islam that exists today.

In the first three decades after his death, a series of four successors or "*caliphs*" were elected to lead the Muslim community in the observation of the Quran and the dissemination of the faith. All were original followers and companions of Muhammed but only the fourth Caliph, **Ali**, Muhammed's cousin and son-in-law was a blood relative.

While the **Sunnis**, or followers of the *sunna* (custom) of the prophet, believed any righteous Muslim could be elected Caliph, the **Shi'as** felt that only descendants of the Prophet had the right to head the *Umma* (legion of followers), and that only Ali could therefore be considered a legitimate successor to Muhammed.

The schism was definitive after Ali's death and the murder of his younger son, **Husayn**. The Sunnis began recognizing the authority of the **Umayyad Dynasty** of elected Caliphs while the **Shi'as** (or "faction") deemed the Umayyads usurpers and began exalting their own line of "spiritually inspired" leaders called *imams*.

SUFISM

Among the Sunnis and Shi'as grew another movement of highly spiritual individuals, "Sufis," who rejected attachments to earthly things and material possessions to cultivate more virtuous relationships with God. As a gesture of ascetic self-denial, many of the early Sufis wore clothes made from

---

[3] For more on Islam see Roraback, Islam in a Nutshell, Enisen Publishing, 2004

coarse wood or *suf* (which gave them their name), and lived simple, austere lives in imitation of Muhammed and the first Caliphs.

For many of them, even the human language was too worldly to describe such a deep sense of spirituality. They resorted to allegorical and symbolic interpretations of the Quran or used music or dance to bring them closer to God.

The Sufis and their *pirs* (holy men), were respected by non-Muslims for their gentle nature and great spiritual awareness and they, in turn, were tolerant of other creeds. These qualities made them effective missionaries. It was the Sufis, in fact, who were most responsible for the spread of the Islam to India (especially the areas that later became Pakistan and Bangladesh) rather than the invading armies of Muslim Arabs.

Although the practice of Sufism has greatly declined in Pakistan, the contribution of the mystic missionaries played a vital role in the country's cultural development.

ISLAM IN PAKISTAN
It was during the expansion of Islam during the **Umayyad Dynasty** of Caliphs (A.D. 661-750) that the subcontinent had its first introduction to Islam. In A.D. 709 Arab naval troops under **Mohammed bin Qasim** landed on the coast of Sindh and promoted the religion as they made their way north.

Although the invaders won some converts, Islam didn't take hold in the region until much later, in part because the ruling Hindu **Brahmins** were permitted to retain their posts in the administration of the country and the local Hindu traditions were respected.

When the Baghdad **Abbasid Caliphs** (A.D. 750-1258) replaced the Umayyads, Islamic and Arabic customs and manners began to influence the Sindhi population. At the same time, Islam was making inroads in the north via Pathan missionaries and was beginning to spread throughout India via the Sufis.

As the **Abbasid Empire** declined, **Mahmud**, son of a former Turkish slave who had become ruler of **Ghazni** (in modern-day Afghanistan), established his own Turkish Empire that extended from Iraq into Punjab. From the beginning of the 11th century, the Ghaznavids and their successors, the **Ghorids** (1148-1206) and then the **Delhi Sultans** converted the masses to Islam by the sword.

The last Delhi Sultan was himself defeated in 1526 by the first in a line of

Muslim emperors of India known as the **Moghuls**. Although the greatest of the Moghul emperors, **Akbar** (1556-1605) was open to and protective of other faiths (particularly Hinduism), Islam dominated as the state religion. The Moghul Empire crumbled after the death of its most pious ruler, **Aurangzeb** (1658-1707), who had adhered to strict Islamic principles and discriminated against non-Muslims.

RELIGION AND THE BRITISH

With the arrival of the British, Moghul society and Islamic culture took a back seat to westernization and Hindu dominance. The Hindus more quickly assimilated to British ways and began to emerge as the prominent force in the subcontinent after their arrival. The status of the Muslims eroded further after they were blamed for a mutiny against the colonists in 1857.

To aggravate matters, the British played on the competitive antagonism between the Muslim and Hindu communities in order to neutralize political movements against the state. The 1885 **Indian National Congress,** which claimed to represent all Indians but maintained an anti-Muslim bias, was counterbalanced by the creation of the **All-India Muslim League** in 1906. After Hindu militants targeted the Muslim majority in Bengal, the Muslim League declared that "Islam was in danger" and began to entertain the "two-nation theory" whereby Hindus and Muslims would have separate spheres of influence on the subcontinent.

ISLAM AND PAKISTAN POLITICS

Pakistan's early leaders were products of the western, secular tradition of the British government and hence envisioned the new country of Pakistan as a state born from Islam but tolerant of all faiths. However, after the death in 1948 of **Mohammed Ali Jinnah,** who had studied law in England and was married to a non-practicing Muslim woman, the question of religion loomed large.

To secularists, the fact that Pakistan was deemed a "Muslim homeland" was enough to guarantee Muslims the liberty to worship. Others believed that Pakistan's *raison d'etre* was to be a model Muslim country ruled by Islamic institutions and Islamic ideas. In many cases, the faith was used to bind the disparate country under a common ideology or as a political tool to legitimize authority.

Liaquat Ali Khan, Pakistan's first Prime Minister after partition, initially followed the secular tradition of the Muslim League and Governor General Jinnah by declaring that non-Muslims would be protected and given complete freedom to practice their religions.

After Jinnah's death, however, the unrest in East Bengal, Sindh and

Pakistan in a Nutshell

Balochistan over what was perceived to be Punjabi domination forced **Liaquat Khan** to change his course and look towards Islam to bring the state together.

Religious clerics once ignored by Jinnah were now invited to participate in the making of the country's constitution and given veto power against any legislation they believed contradicted Islamic law.

The influence of the clerics was tempered, however, with the installation of **Ghulam Mohammed** in 1951 as Governor General. Ghulam Mohammed and his supporters (**Iskander Mirza** and **General Ayub Khan** among them) believed that religion and politics should remain separate in Pakistan, especially since Islam—which was practiced by the vast majority of the population— was no longer under threat from Hindu dominance.

Ghulam Mohammed's successor, **Iskander Mirza**, further believed that an emphasis on religious exclusivity would exacerbate the differences that already existed in the country among the Sunnis, Shi'ites, Ahmedis and a sizeable Hindu minority in East Pakistan.

After the demoralizing loss of Bangladesh in 1971, the role of Islam as a cohesive element was again emphasized. At first, **President Z. A. Bhutto** (1971-77) tried to reestablish a sense of national unity through his **Pakistan People's Party** (PPP) platform of populism and socialism, which he equated with Islamic principles of equality.

Bhutto's critics, however, deemed the PPP platform Western and un-Islamic. Although Bhutto tried to counter their claims by adopting Islamic measures such as the prohibition of alcohol, gambling and nightclubs, and promising to introduce **Sharia (or Shariat)** laws (see People and Policies), his regime fell to the ultra-Islamic command of **General Mohammed Zia ul-Haq** (1977-1988).

Zia, who drew most of his support from Islamic religious parties, rose to power on the wave of anti-Bhutto sentiment and the allegation that the former Prime Minster's last 1977 landslide victory was rigged. He spent the rest of his term trying to legitimize his coup and his subsequent rule. Appealing to the religious sentiments of his constituents, Zia claimed that Allah had provided him an opportunity to serve Islam as a ruler. He further declared that he was committed to transforming the country's economic and political structure according to the principles of Islam.

Among Zia's reforms, **Shariat Courts** were introduced in 1979 to determine whether existing laws were in line with Islamic precepts, and political parties were outlawed. The existing political system was deemed un-Islamic and Muslims were instructed to share their wealth through Muslim *zakat* and *ushr* taxes. Zia also enacted the **Hudood Ordinance of Behavioral Crimes against Islam** and the **Islamic Code** was named the Supreme Law of the land. According to **Shariat** (Islamic law), theft was punishable by amputation, adulteresses were to be stoned and the penalty for speaking blasphemously against the Prophet Muhammed was execution. Although such severe sentences were not regularly carried out, Pakistanis could face legal punishment for violating Islamic codes of conduct such as drinking alcohol or gambling. The effects of Zia's reforms continue to resonate to this day.

When the Soviets invaded Afghanistan in 1979, Zia's position as protector of Islam was strengthened even more. As Pakistan supported the *mujahideen* (holy warriors) who had joined to fight the infidel communist Soviets, Zia's credibility and image in the world's Muslim nations soared until his death in 1988.

Ghulam Ishaq, who was quickly installed as President after Zia's death in a plane crash, was uneasy with the vigorous drive toward Islamization. His aim was to return the country to conventional, secular politics as soon as possible and he ordered the nation to proceed with the elections that had long been promised by the late President.

The election of 36-year-old **Benazir Bhutto**, daughter of **Z. A. Bhutto** and the first woman in modern history to head the government of a Muslim nation, showed that the country's populace didn't agree with Zia's Islamic fundamentalism. Bhutto's gender, though, prevented her from winning the support of the country's religious right.

Prime Minister **Nawaz Sharif**, Benazir Bhutto's successor, attempted to bridge the gap between Pakistan's secular groups and religious adherents by blending capitalist elements with Islamic tenets. He addressed the need to alter the banking system to conform to Islamic laws by eliminating monetary interest (*riba*) for example, while complying with the internationally accepted system of banking abroad. In 1991 he passed a **Sharia Bill** through the National Assembly that exposed and then nullified a number of existing federal and provincial laws that were found to be antithetical to Islam. The move prompted secularist to charge that he was trying to turn Pakistan into a theocratic state. At the same time, Sharif was criticized by the fundamentalists for what they perceived to be his weak commitment to Islamic principles.

The current president, **Pervez Musharraf**, believed that religious fundamentalism and a narrow education system caused Muslim countries to lag far behind the developed world economically and technologically. To help bring the country out its "darkness" the General worked to modernize

Pakistan's schools (especially the *madrassas*) and to curb religious extremist activity by banning the most militant groups and detaining fundamentalist leaders.

The religious right, which viewed his actions as a step towards turning Pakistan into a completely secular state, accused the General of being a puppet of the Western powers, especially in light of Musharraf's cooperation with the United States in the war with Afghanistan. To fight for their cause politically, the mainstream religious parties (including **Jamaat-i-Islami**, **Jamiat Ulema-e-Pakistan** and others) collaborated to form the **Mutahidda Majilis-e-Amal** (MMA United Action Front) to run against the moderates in the October 2002 general elections.

In June 2003, the local government of Pakistan's North West Frontier Province became the first in Pakistan to be run by Sharia Law. The province, which is led by an alliance of six Islamic parties led by the MMA, voted to enforce Taliban-like fundamentalist government in the region and has become a sanctuary for Afghan rebels fighting the U.S. forces in eastern Afghanistan.

SHI'A/SUNNI SECTARIAN VIOLENCE

In terms of the Islamic faith, **Shi'a** (Shi'ite) and **Sunni** Muslims share many fundamental similarities. Both believe that Mohammed was the last prophet of God (Allah) and both observe the **Five Pillars of Islam**. But their differences are significant enough to have caused upheavals resulting in the deaths of thousands of people.

Minority Shi'as, for example, tend to worship in their own mosques and have their own clerical leaders and ceremonies. They also maintain some of their own distinct customs and legal codes including laws of tithing and taxation. Shi'as, for instance, believe tithes like *zakat* and *ushr* should be given directly to the needy rather than funneled through the state.

When **President Zia ul-Haq** implemented obligatory state collection of the *zakat* and *ushr* taxes (state-ordered tithes) as part of his Islamization plan, the Shi'as rose in revolt. Although the religious minority was eventually exempted from paying the tax, the damage had been done. The *zakat* issue provoked violent demonstrations in Pakistani neighborhoods for the next several years.

The Islamic revolution in predominantly Shi'a Iran in the late 1970s further exacerbated hostilities between the Shi'as and Sunnis. At that time, the slightly more empowered Shi'as of Pakistan founded the **Tehrik-e-Jafria** ("Movement of Followers of Shi'a") led by a student leader of Iran's **Ayatollah Khomeini**, prompting radical Sunnis to join the extremist **Sipah-e-Sahaba**. Both parities were banned in January 2002.

The assassination of Sipah-e-Sahaba's founder, **Maulana Jhangvi** in 1990 caused an upsurge of sectarian violence in the country and led to the formation of a breakaway and more radical group called **Lashkar-e-Jhangvi** (which was banned by Musharraf in 2001).

AHMADIS (AHMEDIS)

While the Shi'as and Sunnis share the fundamental belief that Muhammed was the last and greatest of all prophets, the followers of the **Ahmadiyya Movement,** who also considered themselves Muslim, believed that another prophet had been born in the 19th century. In the same way that Jesus had followed Moses and Muhammad followed Moses, the Ahmadis believed their founder, **Hazrat Mirza Ghulam Ahmad** (1835-1908), was sent by God as the promised Messiah (*Mahdi*) to help fulfill the laws that had been revealed to Muhammed more than thirteen centuries earlier. To the Sunni and Shi'a Muslims, the Punjab-based Ahmadis were heretics since they violated the first pillar of Islam by denying that Muhammed was the final Prophet of God.

In the first decade of Pakistan's existence, violent mobs of anti-Ahmadi rioters insisted that all followers of that faith, including those who had held important positions in the military and the government after Partition (including Pakistan's first foreign minister) be deemed non-Muslims and stripped of their privileges.

Conceding to mob pressure, the Ahmadis were formally decertified as Muslims during **Z. A. Bhutto's** regime and henceforth prevented from ever holding the office of president or prime minister in the country. With the implementation of **Martial Law Ordinance XX** in 1984, moreover, the Ahmadis were branded as criminals liable to fines and imprisonment if they posed as Muslims or used Islamic terms when practicing their beliefs.

In 1993, when members of the **Ahmadiyya Movement** complained in Pakistan's court that they were being deprived of their religious rights and freedoms as guaranteed under **Article 20** of the constitution, the Supreme Court countered that Islamic phrases were, in effect copyrighted trademarks of the Islamic faith. Use of these phrases by Ahmadis, the court concluded, was therefore a form of copyright infringement.

Until recently, the Ahmadis and all other non-Muslim minorities were only permitted to hold 10 of 217 seats in Pakistan's Parliament. Musharraf did away with the "separate electorate system" in early 2002.

PAKISTAN PENAL CODE FOR BLASPHEMY
295-B   Whoever defiles damages or desecrates a copy of the Quran shall be punished by imprisonment for life.
295-C   Any person who directly or indirectly, by imputation, innuendo or insinuation defiles the sacred name of the Holy Prophet shall be punished by death or imprisonment for life.
298-A   Use of derogatory remarks in respect to holy personages (i.e. any wife or member of the Prophet's family or any of the Righteous Caliphs or companions of the Prophet) shall be punished by up to three years in prison or fine or both.
298-C   Persons of the **Qadiani group** (**Ahmadis**) who call themselves Muslims or refer to their faith as Islam shall be subject to up to three years in prison and a fine.

Blasphemy laws were enacted by the British in India in order to keep Muslims, Hindus and Sikhs from using inflammatory religious slurs that could trigger communal violence. To please Pakistan's religious parties, President **Zia ul-Haq** changed the nature of the laws in Pakistan to protect Islam alone.

Since an act of blasphemy must be considered intentional to merit punishment, say proponents of the laws, blasphemy charges cannot be made against Christians or other non-Muslim minorities who are practicing their faiths privately or in their own places of worship. Islamic leaders also say the laws keep peace since they deter mobs from delivering vigilant justice to dissenters.

So far no one has been executed for blasphemy although high profile cases, such as the death sentence against **Dr. Younus Sheikh,** an allopathic physician and member of the International Humanist and Ethical Union, have attracted negative attention from International Human Rights organizations. Critics have also have claimed that the laws have been abused by opportunists seeking to malign their rivals by accusing them of committing blasphemous acts.

MADRASSAS

Madrassas, or Islamic religious schools, have been educating Muslim students since the time of Muhammed. But while the ancient *madrassas* were once lauded for their enlightened and progressive curricula, madrassas today have been criticized for producing narrow-minded fundamentalist terrorists. The truth is somewhere in between.

Most of Pakistan's madrassas do have strong religious inclinations and teach their students Islamic subjects like Quranic law, Arabic (in order to read the Quran in its original language), and the ways of the Prophet. And some, like the **Haqqania School**, have an anti-western, militant agenda. But their popularity and success are mostly due to their accessibility by orphans and students whose families could not otherwise afford to send their sons to school.

Madrassas, unlike state and secular institutions, receive most of their funding from external sources: wealthy Arab or Asian benefactors, for instance, or earned income from the schools' own investments. In turn they offer students a tuition-free education, free room and board, school supplies, clothes and often stipends. Pashto-speaking refugees form Afghanistan also flocked to madrassas that taught courses in their own language.

The schools were in great demand in the 1970s and 80s during **Zia ul-Haq's** Islamization drive and throughout the *jihad* (holy war) against the Soviet infidels in Afghanistan that attracted pious Muslim fighters from around the world. In the last few years the schools have become hotbeds of controversy because of their support for the extremist Taliban regime that took over after the civil war that followed Soviet withdrawal.

Sami ul-Haq, the son of **Abdul Haq**, the founder and director of the **Haqqania School**, one of the largest *madrassas* in the country, boasted that 90% of the Taliban's ruling elite graduated from his madrassa and that his students received extra credit for fighting Taliban rival **Ahmed Shah Masoud** in 1999. He is also believed to be one of **Osama bin Laden's** closest friends.

Because of the Taliban's close relationship with **Osama bin Laden**, the accused mastermind behind terrorist attacks in New York City on September 11, 2001, and other incidents of terror associated with madrassa students, the current regime saw the need to curb extremist activities by modernizing the school system.

In December, 2001, General Pervez Musharraf announced that his government would boost funding to Islamic schools that adopted modern subjects, like science, computers, English and math, and cut off funds to those schools believed to breed violent activity.

Madrassa supporters have predicted that any move taken against the schools would provoke fundamentalist uprisings against the government or, at best, would have little effect since most schools do not rely on state grants collected from *zakat* taxes.

POLITICS

In 1980, a group of center and left-wing parties led by the **PPP** (the "Pakistan People's Party" headed by **Benazir Bhutto**) formed the **Movement for the Restoration of Democracy** (MRD) which demanded the resignation of **President General Zia ul-Haq**, new elections and the restoration of the Constitution. Their objectives were finally realized in 1988 when President Zia was killed in a plane crash and the country was returned to full representative democracy after 11 years of military rule.

Since 1988, more than 100 political parties have competed for seats in Pakistan's parliament, the *Majilis-e-Shura*, either as members of political coalitions or independently. Polls, however, were usually dominated by the PPP and the **PML** ("Pakistan Muslim League" led by **Nawaz Sharif**).

In order to break the hold of the leading parties, the regime of **Pervez Musharraf** backed a new faction of the PML, called the **PML/Quaid-i-Azam** faction (also called the "**King's Party**" by opponents).

Also emerging in 2002 was the **MMA** (Muttahida Mahaz-e-Amal), a coalition of about a dozen Muslim parties with anti-Western, pro-Islamic sentiments.

PARLIAMENT
Pakistan has a bi-cameral (two house) parliament or *Majilis-e-Shura* consisting of a Senate and a National Assembly.

Senate (next election 2006)
100 seats. Members indirectly elected by local assemblies to serve 4-year terms.

National Assembly (next election 2006)
342 seats – 60 seats allocated to women, 10 seats given to minorities. Members are elected by popular vote to serve 4-year terms.

President (next election 2007)
Elected by Parliament for a 5-year term

Prime Minister (next election 2006)
Elected by the National Assembly for a 4-year term

RESULTS 2002 ELECTIONS
Senate results Feb. 2002:
PML/Q 40, PPP/P 11, MMA 21, MQM/A 6, PML/N 4, NA 3, PML/F 1, PkMAP 2, ANP 2, PPP/S 2, JWP 1, BNP-Awami 1, BNP-Mengal 1, BNM/H 1, independents 4

National Assembly results Oct. 2002:
PML/Q 117, PPP/P 81, MMA 60, PML/N 19, MQM/A 17, NA 16, PML/F 5, PML/J 3, PPP/S 2, BNP 1, JWP 1, PAT 1, PML/Z 1, PTI 1, MQM/H 1, PkMAP 1, PSPP 1, independent candidates 15.

POLITICAL PARTIES

ANP		Awami National Party (Wali Khan)
BNM/H		Balochistan National Movement/Hayee Group
BNM/M		Balochistan National Movement/Mengal Group
BNP		Balochi National Party
BNP/Awami		Baluch National Party/Awami
BNP/Mengal		Baluch National Party/Mengal
JWP		Jamhoori Watan Party (Akbar Khan Bugti)
MMA		Muttahida Majilis-e-Amal Pakistan - umbrella org. incl:
	JAH	Jamiat-e-Ahle Hadith
	JI	Jamaat-i-Islami
	JUP	Jamiat Ulema-e-Pakistan
	JUI/S	Jamiat Ulema-i-Islam, Sami ul Haq faction
	TEI	Tehrik-e Islami
	TJP	Tehrik-i-Jafria Pakistan
MQM/A		Muttahida Qaumi Movement, Altaf faction
MQM/H		Muttahida Qaumi Movement, Haquiqi faction
NA		National Alliance
PkMAP		Pathan Khwa Milli Awami Party
PAT		Pakistan Awami Tehrik
PML/F		Pakistan Muslim League, Functional Group
PML/J		Pakistan Muslim League, Junejo faction
PML/N		Pakistan Muslim League, Nawaz Sharif faction
PML/Q		Pakistan Muslim League, Quaid-i-Azam faction
PML/Z		Pakistan Muslim League, Zia-ul Haq
PPP/P		Pakistan People's Party, Parliamentarians
PPP/S		Pakistan People's Party, Sherpao
PTI		Pakistan Tehrik-e-Insaaf

PML (Pakistan Muslim League)

Founded in Dacca (Dakha) India in 1906, the **All-India Muslim League** was created to promote the cause of Muslims in the Indian subcontinent who were underrepresented in the Hindu-dominated **Indian National Congress.** The Muslim League and Congress agreed to combine their efforts in 1916 (the **Lucknow Pact**) to work towards independence from Britain. But the collaboration fell apart after Muslim League president, **Mohammed Ali Jinnah**, became disillusioned with Hindu **Mahatma Ghandi's** methods and left the country. When he returned from England in 1935, he reinvigorated the Muslim League with a new agenda – the creation of a separate Muslim state (Pakistan).

The Muslim League continued to play a major role in the country after independence until **Zia ul-Haq** declared all political parties un-Islamic in 1986. However, by that time, the party's original purpose of creating Pakistan had already been achieved and the League's ranks were filled with Punjabi landlords and bureaucrats who were more concerned with increasing their personal influence than building a strong national organization. Divisions and policy changes had altered the party so significantly that it had become a far cry from the party that founded the nation.

Politicians like President **Ayub Khan**, who formed a party called the **Pakistan Muslim League** (PML) in 1962, and **Mohammed Khan Junejo**, who established the **PML-J** (for Junejo), drew on the Muslim League's distinction as Pakistan's inaugural political party to strengthen claims of legitimacy and authenticity. When **Nawaz Sharif** took over the party in 1993, it became the **PML-N** (Nawaz).

After years of dominance in Pakistan's parliament, the PML-N weakened after its leader, former Prime Minister **Nawaz Sharif**, was exiled to Saudi Arabia on charges of hijacking then-Chief of Army Staff General Musharraf's plane in 1999.

In Sharif's absence, a small group of PML-N members challenged the monopoly that Nawaz Sharif and his family had held over the party for years by forming their own party, the **PML/Quaid-i-Azam faction** (or PML/Q) led by **Mian Azhar**. Sometimes called the **"King's Party"** because of the strong backing from **President General Musharraf**, the Punjab-based PML/Q was considered moderate and progressive and its leadership generally agreed with the President's policies on Afghanistan and Kashmir.

PPP (PAKISTAN PEOPLE'S PARTY)

Formed in October 1967 by **Zulfikar Ali Bhutto**, who was elected Chairman, the PPP was the only party since the Muslim League to have been established as a mass political party. Despite its slogan, "Islam our Faith, Democracy our Polity, Socialism our Economy, All Powers to the People," the PPP did little to advance the first two tenets, Islam and Democracy, and concentrated on its socialist program of land reforms and nationalization which alienated industrialists and entrepreneurs.

The middle class also argued that the PPP's populist platform of "bread, clothing and shelter," which appealed to the poor masses, was accomplished at the expense of the bourgeoisie. The religious right also complained about the party's disregard for Islamic issues.

After Z. A. Bhutto's death, his wife and daughter managed PPP affairs until **Benazir Bhutto's** rise to power in 1988. Under her leadership, the party abandoned most references to socialism and focused instead on the party's democratic character, especially in contrast to the autocratic tendencies of President Zia ul-Haq and Prime Minister Nawaz Sharif.

In 2002, the party was forced to run under an altered name. The new party, calling itself the PPP-Parliamentarians (PPP/P) was headed by **Amin Makhdoom Fahim** and included virtually all PPP leaders.

Benazir Bhutto, who has been living in self-imposed exile since 1998 in order to avoid arrest in Pakistan on corruption charges, was barred from participating in the elections.

MMA (Muttahida Mahaz-e-Amal)

With the leaders of the main opposition parties (Bhutto and Sharif) in exile and following global trends towards Islamicism, the focus of Pakistan politics has shifted away from secular debates towards religious interests. In 2002, consequently, a new coalition of Islamic parties emerged and won a significant number of seats in Pakistan's parliament.

The MMA (Muttahida Mahaz-e-Amal) represents all the major Islamic sects in the country including Maulana Fazlur Rahman's **Jamaat Ulema-e-Islami** (JUI/F), Maulana Sami ul-Haq's **Jamaat Ulema-e-Pakistan** (JUP) , the Shi'a party **Tehrik-i-Islami** and the sectarian **Jamaat Islami** (JI) among others.

The party has won much appeal from lower-middle class constituents through the persuasion of religious Mullahs operating in local mosques and madrassas. However, the same attributes that have attracted Pakistanis — the party's anti-Western, pro-Sharia stance – is also distressing to the international community.

Internal conflicts between different Islamic sects and among its leaders also threaten to weaken the party. In order to impose a pure Islamic state based on Sharia law, for instance, the leaders of the MMA would have to agree on an Islamic ideology (Shi'a or Sunni, Deobandi or Barelvi etc.). The leaders of JI and JUI also disagree on the party's relationship to the ruling regime and the situation in Kashmir (JUI favors rapprochement with India, JI opposes it).

Other Pakistani constituents are also fearful that the religious parties have concentrated too heavily on spiritual issues (banning liquor and gambling, trying to enact Sharia Law, censoring billboards, for instance) and have neglected to address the basic concerns of the people (education, employment, sanitation, roads etc.).

MQM (MUTAHI QAUMI MOVEMENT)

The Mutahi Qaumi Movement (formerly Mohajir Qaumi Movement) was formed in 1984 (politically active in 1986) to defend the interest of the *Mohajirs*, Muslim refugees from India. The party's founder, **Altaf Hussain** (in self-exile in London) hoped to give the immigrant community a political voice in Pakistan's Punjabi-dominated government.

The MQM party became less effective after it split into factions, the **Altaf Hussain** group (MQM/A) and the splinter **anti-Altaf Hussain** faction, which called itself the **MQM Haquiqi** or "real" MQM. The Altaf Hussein group itself was divided into Sunni and Shi'a factions purportedly due to interference by the Inter-Services Intelligence (see <u>ISI</u>) in an attempt to diminish the party's solidarity and influence.

MUSLIM EXTREMISM

Pakistan's rise in Islamic militant activity in the last quarter century can be traced to the Muslim world's *jihad* (holy war) against the Soviets in Afghanistan in the 1980s and the subsequent build up of troops of *mujahideen* (holy warriors) in the area.

After the war, the trained freedom fighters were left without a battle to fight and were abandoned by their former ally, the United States. Many of the *mujahideen* redirected their energies to fight *jihads* being waged in Pakistan's disputed Kashmir territory or other parts of the world (i.e. Chechnya) and to the preservation of Islam in the face of hostile elements from India, the West, or even liberals within Pakistan.

Many of these *mujahideen*, who had assembled into extremist organizations, received protection and support from Pakistan's government agencies because they appeared to share Pakistan's national goals – for example, maintaining strong ties with Afghanistan and breaking India's grip on Kashmir. That is, until Pervez Musharraf's rise to power in 1999 and the realization that these fertile groups could turn against Pakistan to create a Taliban-style system of government.

Musharraf began cracking down on militant activity in 1999 and stepped up activity after the terrorist attacks in New York in 2001. When war with India loomed after Pakistani terrorists were implicated in a bomb attack on India's parliament building in December 2001, General Musharraf banned five militant groups and rounded up thousands of people suspected of having ties to terrorist groups. At the same time he announced reforms on hard-line religious schools (*madrassas*) which had become training grounds for Islamic fundamentalists.

Banned Jan. 2002: Lashkar-e-Toiba, Jaish-e-Mohammed, Sipah-e-Sahaba, Tehrik-e-Jafria, Tanzeem-e-Nifaz-e-Shariat-e-Mohammedi

Many groups continued to operate after the ban under different names.

KASHMIRI MILITANT GROUPS
HARKAT ANSAR
Harkat Ansar is an Inter Services Intelligence-backed guerrilla faction that fought in the Afghan war against Soviet occupation in the 1980s.

HARKAT UL-MUJAHIDEEN (HUM) - RENAMED JAMIAT UL-ANSAR
Banned by Musharraf in January 2002 **Leader is Fazlur Rehman Khalil**
HUM, which grew out of Harkat Ansar, operates primarily in Kashmir and runs terrorist training camps in Afghanistan. In 1998 its commander, Farooq

Kashmiri, signed Osama bin Laden's *fatwa* (Islamic declaration) calling for attacks on American and Western interests.

In 1999, the group negotiated the liberation of **Maula Masood Azhar**, an imprisoned former leader of Harkat, in exchange for the release of passengers held hostage on a hijacked Indian Airlines flight. When Azhar was set free, he formed his own party, the **Jaish-e-Mohammed.**

JAISH-E-MOHAMMED (JeM) also known as KHUDDAM-UL-ISLAM (KHUDDAMUL ISLAM) and TEHRIK UL-FURQAAN.
JeM, which wants Indian-occupied Kashmir to merge with Pakistan, was blamed for the December 2001 attack on India's Parliament building. Musharraf detained the party's founder, Maula Masood Azhar, in January 2002.

HEZB-UL-MUJAHIDEEN (Hizbul Mujahideen)
Hezb ul-Mujahideen, a much larger Kashmir separatist group than Harkat ul- Mujahideen, has not yet been banned since it is not a Paksitan based organization, but its leader has been accused of carrying out several terrorist attacks and their activities have been restricted.

LASHKAR-E-TAJEBBA (Lashkar-e-Toiba) (LeT)
LeT, along with JeM, was blamed for the suicide attacks on India's parliament. The group has been fighting to merge the Indian part of Kashmir with Pakistan and is also connected with Bin Laden and his *fatwa* against the West. LeT's leader has also been linked to several terrorist operations and is under detention in Pakistan.

The groups agenda goes beyond merely challenging Indian rule in Kashmir. In a pamphlet titled "Why are we waging jihad" the group defined its agenda as restoring Islamic rule over all parts of India.

SECTARIAN MILITANT GROUPS
SIPAH-E-SAHABA (SSP)
Sipah-e-Sahaba, a radical anti-Shi'a group, was founded by the Sunni cleric **Maulana Haq Nawaz Jhangvi** in the 1980s and carried as its platform the desire to officially declare Pakistan a Sunni Muslim state to be ruled by Shar'ia law. Among its infamous members were **Ramzi Yousef** (one of the main suspects in the 1993 New York World Trade Center explosion) and **Abu Musab al-Zarqawi**.(regarded as the most lethal Sunni insurgent in Iraq).

In 1990, **Jhangvi** was assassinated – allegedly by a Shi'a terrorist group and in August 2001, the party was officially banned by the government of Pervez Musharraf. Many of its members then joined the Taliban in Afghanistan.

LASHKAR-E-JHANGVI (LEJ)

In 1996, a group of militants broke from the SSP because they believed the sectarian party had deviated too far from founder, Jhangvi's, militant ideals. The new party, Lashkar-e-Jhangvi, proved to be even more radical than its predecessor and was implicated in the deaths of 25 Shiite Muslims in 1998, found responsible for a 2003 attack on a Shiite mosque in Quetta and blamed for murdering US oil workers. Most notably, members of Lashkar-e-Jhangvi were believed to have participated in the kidnapping and murder of Wall Street Journal reporter **Daniel Pearl** in early 2002.

Also in 2002, **Lashkar-e-Jhangvi** entered into a loose coalition with radical Kashmiri militant groups **Harkat-ul-Jihad-i-Islami** (JuJI) and **Jaish-e-Mohammed** to form **Lashkar-e-Omar** (LeO) (possibly named after Taliban leader Mullah Mohammed Omar). The association gave the party a significant boost in its influence and power.

In January 2003, LeJ, which is believed to be connected with Al-Qaeda, was designated a foreign terrorist organization by the US.

TEHRIK-E-JAFRIA "Followers of Shi'a sect" (TeJ)

TeJ was founded in 1979 at the peak of Zia's Islamization drive and during the Islamic revolution in primarily Shi'a Iran.

TANZEEM-E-NIFAZ-E-SHARIAT-E-MOHAMMEDI

This radical Sunni Muslim group reportedly sent members to Afghanistan to help the Taliban. Its founder, **Maulana Sufi Mohammed**, a follower of the Wahhabi school, was detained by Musharraf in 2002.

NUCLEAR WAR AND SANCTIONS

The specter of war between Pakistan and India over the disputed territory of Kashmir has been especially troubling since each country has exhibited the nuclear capability to obliterate the other.

Initially, India began its nuclear program to counter China after India's defeat in a 1962 border war with the Asian country. The US, heavily involved in a Cold war against communism at the time, welcomed India's role as a potential counterweight to Red China and the Soviet Union and even supplied the subcontinent nation with nuclear technology. In a written statement, India claimed that the plutonium furnished by the US and Canada would be used solely for "peaceful purposes" and detonated its first and only "peaceful nuclear explosion," in 1974 under the same guise.

Pakistan, meanwhile, recovering from its own defeat by India in 1971, declared that it, too, would develop the capacity to make atomic weapons even if the financial cost would require its citizens to "eat grass." President **Zulfikar Ali Bhutto**, who recognized the political advantages of pursuing Pakistan's popular quest for a nuclear device, declared that his country would build the first "Islamic bomb."

Bhutto's successor, **Mohammed Zia ul-Haq**, continuing where Bhutto left off, claimed that his country finally had the capability to build the Bomb. Pakistan was subsequently beset with economic and military sanctions in observance of the **Symington Amendment** to the Foreign Assistance Act of 1961 (see Terms below).

The Soviet invasion of Afghanistan in 1979, however, brought on a drastic change in international policy. From 1981-1990 sanctions were waived and western aid to Pakistan skyrocketed to reward the country for its help in repelling the Soviets.

The 1985 **Pressler Amendment** sanctions, which banned economic and military assistance to Pakistan as long as the country possessed nuclear devices, were imposed at the war's end in 1990 after Pakistan had lost its strategic significance.

Eight years later, India detonated five test nuclear devises 60 miles from the border of Pakistan. Pakistan followed suit a few weeks later despite then-US President **Bill Clinton's** offer of conventional weaponry and financial aid if Islamabad didn't carry out the tests. Pakistan's Prime Minister **Nawaz Sharif** explained that any reluctance on his part to detonate nuclear devices would surely cause his constituents to drive him out of office. Pakistan, whose economy was more reliant on international loans than India, faced the dual cost of sanctions and a potential nuclear arms race until the **Symington** and **Pressler Amendments** sanctions were waived in September 2001 after the terrorist attacks on New York and Washington.

Pakistan in a Nutshell

Like the US and USSR during the Cold War, India and Pakistan possess enough weapons to cause **mutual assured destruction (MAD)**. Unlike the two superpowers, though, neither Pakistan nor India has maintained adequate safeguards, such as spy satellites to watch each other's weapons or a hotline for communication between leaders during a crisis, to prevent an accidental nuclear war.

Under the **Nuclear Non-Proliferation Treaty (NPT),** Nuclear Weapons States are prohibited from assisting other nations "in any way" with their nuclear weaponry. Countries like the United States, therefore, can only help India and Pakistan develop safeguards if or when they are accepted as full-fledged nuclear countries in their own right.

Alternatively, the United States and other NPT countries can continue the policy of economic sanctions in hopes that India and Pakistan will calculate that the diplomatic and financial costs of sanctions outweigh the advantages of having nuclear weapons, as did South Africa, Belarus, Ukraine, Libya and other countries. India shelved its own plans for an underground nuclear test in 1983 and 1995 because of sanctions.

Despite strong American pressure, neither India nor Pakistan has so far signed the **Non-Proliferation Treaty** or **Comprehensive Test Ban treaty**.

ABDUL QADEER KHAN
A month after the September 11, 2001 attacks on the New York City World Trade Center, the Pakistan government arrested three Pakistani nuclear scientists for their suspected connections with the Taliban. All three had been associated with Pakistan's national hero, **Abdul Qadeer Khan**, the "father of Pakistan's bomb."

Two years later, it was discovered that the nuclear scientist, **A.Q. Khan,** had passed on designs and technology for building nuclear weapons to North Korea, Iran and Libya among other countries. Khan's confession in January 2004 posed a political dilemma for President Musharraf who already faced accusations of being too pro-American. Imposing a tough sentence on the national hero would likely result in rioting in Pakistan. No punishment, on the other hand, would give the appearance of government complicity to the West.

TERMS
Symington Amendment to the Foreign Assistance Act of 1961
Prohibits US economic and military assistance to any country delivering or receiving nuclear enrichment equipment, material or technology not safeguarded by the International Atomic Energy Agency.

Pressler Amendment to the Foreign Assistance Act of 1961
States that no assistance (militarily or technologically) shall be given to Pakistan unless the president certifies that Pakistan does not possess nuclear weapons.

ISI

Sometimes labeled Pakistan's "secret army," "rogue agency" and "invisible government, the **Inter-Services Intelligence** (ISI), Pakistan's powerful military intelligence agency, has been accused of supporting some of Pakistan's most radical Islamic militant organizations. The ISI has also been charged with backing the **Taliban,** orchestrating political assassinations, fueling Kashmiri insurgents, smuggling narcotics and procuring nuclear components for the Pakistan government in the half-century of its existence.

Founded in 1948, the agency was initially created to collect external political intelligence, primarily from India and Kashmir. But the role of the ISI expanded to include management of internal affairs first under **General Ayub Khan,** who had the ISI gather information in East Pakistan (now Bangladesh), then with **Zulfikar Ali Bhutto,** who used the agency to monitor Balochi insurrectionists. **Zia ul-Haq** also used the agency to curb rebellious activity in Sindh.

After the successful 1979 revolution in predominantly Shi'a Muslim Iran furthermore, the ISI was employed to monitor and control the activities of Pakistan's Shi'a minority resulting in the formation of a number of anti-Shi'a extremist organizations including the **Sipah-e-Sahaba.**

The ISI also assisted President **Zia** by examining the activity of rival **Benazir Bhutto's PPP** party and allegedly orchestrating the assassination of her brother, **Shah Nawaz Bhutto**, in the French Riviera in 1985.

When Benazir Bhutto won the 1988 election she in turn tried to limit the independent authority of the ISI by installing her own candidate as its director. The ISI retaliated by undermining her regime and contributing to her dismissal in 1990.

The ISI was very tight with Benazir's successor, **Mian Nawaz Sharif,** and played a large part in his efforts to replace then-Chief of Army Staff, General **Pervez Musharraf**. When the army deposed Sharif in 1999, however, Musharraf appointed a new ISI head loyal to himself, Lieutenant-General **Ehsanul Haq**.

ISI AND AFGHANISTAN
The ISI's covert capabilities were greatly enhanced during the war in Afghanistan in the 1980s and with the subsequent alliance between Pakistan and the United States. To help fight the war against the Soviets, America's intelligence agency, the **CIA,** funneled money and arms through the Inter-Services Intelligence agency and trained a number of ISI officers to lead the *mujahideen* (Islamic holy warriors) in their *jihad* (holy war) against the communists.

The ISI continued to play a role in Afghanistan long after the Soviets withdrew in 1989. To reclaim Pakistan's "strategic depth" with regard to India, the intelligence agency initially supported its own candidate, **Gulbuddin Hekmatyar,** to lead Afghanistan after the defeat of the Russians. When Hekmatyar failed to take Kabul from the forces under Defense Minister **Ahmed Shah Massoud**, the ISI began sponsoring a then little-known Pathan group of students called the **Taliban** and provided them with the military and financial support that helped put them in power.

The ISI maintained good relations with the Taliban until the attacks on New York and Washington D.C. on September 11, 2001 when they were instructed by Musharraf's regime to turn their allegiance around full circle to become the watchdogs for the West in Afghanistan during the campaign against suspected terrorist mastermind **Osama bin Laden**.

ISI AND KASHMIR
The ISI also fueled the crisis in Kashmir by covertly training anti-Indian militants and supporting extremist Kashmiri organizations such as **Lashkar-e-Toiba** and **Jaish-e-Mohammed** (both banned by Musharraf).

Hordes of religious fighters were purportedly redirected form Afghanistan after 1989 to Kashmir with promises of glory and money in exchange for fighting a *jihad* (or holy war) against the Indians.

ISI TODAY
In the last few years the agency has had no real supervision and has become a self-governing entity answerable neither to the leadership of the army nor the President or Prime Minister.

Because of **Musharraf's** former position as Chief of Army Staff, it has been predicted that he would be able to assume a stronger hold on the organization than former civilian leaders. Since September 11,2001 Musharraf has appointed a liberal, moderate Director General and has ordered the agency to end its support of the Taliban and Islamic militant groups fighting in Kashmir. Despite these significant changes, the ISI apparatus is believed to be too big, powerful and self-interested to completely transform overnight.

***

Enisen publishing would like to thank the following people for their generous assistance in the development of "Pakistan in a Nutshell":

Former Pakistan Consul General Raana Rahim
Lieutenant Colonel Kent L. Chaplin
Commercial Counselor, Tariq Bajwa
Dr. Aziz Khan
Syud Sharif

For a bibliography and more information about Pakistan, please visit www.enisen.com.

Other Books by Amanda Roraback:
Afghanistan in a Nutshell
Iraq in a Nutshell
Islam in a Nutshell
Israel-Palestine in a Nutshell